DISCARD

Ideas and the Novel

MARY McCARTHY

Ideas
and
the Novel

Harcourt Brace Jovanovich
New York and London

Requests for permission to make copies of
any part of the work should be mailed to:
Permissions, Harcourt Brace Jovanovich,
Inc., 757 Third Avenue, New York, N.Y.,
10017

Northcliffe Lectures,
1980, University College, London

Lectures 1 and 4 were previously published,
in somewhat different form, in the *London
Review of Books.*

Library of Congress Cataloging in Publication Data

McCarthy, Mary Therese, 1912–
Ideas and the novel.
(Northcliffe lectures; 1980)
1. Fiction—History and criticism.
2. Idea (Philosophy) in literature.
I. Title. II. Series:
Northcliffe lectures; 1980.
PN3347.M3   809.3   80-82344
ISBN 0-15-143682-7

Printed in the United States of America

First edition

B C D E

To Sonia Orwell,
with gratitude

Ideas and the Novel

1

"He had a mind so fine that no idea could violate it."

T. S. Eliot writing of Henry James in *The Little Review* of August, 1918. I offer it to you as a motto or, rather, counter-motto for the reflections that follow, which will take exception, not to the truth of Eliot's pronouncement (he was right about James), but to the set of lofty assumptions calmly towering behind it.

The young Eliot's epigram summed up with cutting brevity a creed that for modernists appeared beyond dispute. Implicit in it is the snubbing notion, radical at the time but by now canon doctrine, of the novel as a fine art and of the novelist as an intelligence superior to mere intellect. In this patronizing view, the intellect's crude apparatus was capable only of formulating concepts, which then underwent the process of diffusion, so that by dint of repetition they fell within anybody's reach. The final, cruel fate of an idea was to turn into an *idée reçue*. The power of the novelist insofar as he was a supreme intelligence was to free himself from the work-load of commentary and simply, awesomely, to show: his creation was beyond paraphrase or reduction. As pure work of art, it stood beautifully apart, impervious to the dry rot affecting the brain's constructions and to the welter of factuality.

Thus the separation was perceived as twofold. The reform program for the novel—soon to be promulgated in a position-paper like *Jacob's Room* (1922)—aimed at correcting not only the errors of the old practitioners, who were prone to philosophize in their works, but also the Victorian "slice of life" theory still admitted by Matthew Arnold and later, permissive notions of the novel as a "spongy tract" (Forster) or large loose bag into which anything would fit. Obviously novels of the old, discredited schools—the historical novel, the novel of adventure, the soap-box or pulpit novel—continued and continue to be written despite the lesson of the Master. Indeed they make up a majority, now as before, but having no recognized aesthetic willing to claim them, they tend to be treated by our critical authorities as marginal—examples of backwardness if they come from the East (Solzhenitsyn) or of deliberate archaizing if they come from the

West (say, Iris Murdoch). The pure novel, the quintessential novel, does not acknowledge any family relation with these distant branches. It is a formal, priestly exercise whose first great celebrant was James. The fact that there are no Jamesian novels being produced any more—if there ever were, apart from the Master's own—does not alter the perspective. The Jamesian model remains a standard, an archetype, against which contemporary impurities and laxities are measured.

The importance of James lies not so much in his achievements as in the queerness of them. He did not broaden a way for his successors but closed nearly every exit as with hermetic sealing tape. It is undeniable that this American author, almost single-handed, invented a peculiar new kind of fiction, more refined, more stately, than anything known before, purged, to the limit of possibility, of the gross traditional elements of suspense, physical action, inventory, description of places and persons, apostrophe, moral teaching. When you think of James in the light of his predecessors, you are suddenly conscious of what is not there: battles, riots, tempests, sunrises, the sewers of Paris, crime, hunger, the plague, the scaffold, the clergy, but also minute particulars such as you find in Jane Austen—poor Miss Bates's twice-baked apples, Mr. Collins' "Collins," the comedy of the infinitely small. It cannot have been simply a class limitation or a limitation of experience that intimidated his pen. It was a resolve, very American, to scrape his sacred texts clean of the material factor. And it was no small task he laid on himself, since his novels, even more than most maybe, dealt with material concerns—property and money—and unrolled almost exclusively in the realm of the social, mundane by definition. Nevertheless, he succeeded, this American prodigy. He etherealized the novel beyond its wildest dreams and perhaps etherized it as well.

To take a pleasant example, he managed in *The Spoils of Poynton* to relate a story of a contest for possession of some furniture in immense detail without ever indicating except in the vaguest way what the desirable stuff was. We gather that quite a lot is French—Louis Quinze and Louis Seize are mentioned once each ("the sweetest Louis Seize")—but we also hear of Venetian velvet and of "a great Italian cabinet" in the red room, though with no specifics of place, period, inlays, embossment, and of a little Spanish ivory crucifix. When you think of what Balzac would have made of the opportunity . . . ! Actually *The Spoils of Poynton is* a Balzacian drama done with the merest hints of props and stage setting. James's strategy was to abstract the general noun, furniture, from the particulars of the individual pieces, also referred to as "things." He gives us a universal which we can upholster according to our own taste and antiquarian knowledge.

In short, he gives us an Idea. *The Spoils of Poynton* is not a novel about material tables and chairs; it is a novel about the possession and enjoyment of an immaterial Idea, which could be *any* old furniture, *all* old furniture, beautiful, ugly, or neither—it makes no difference, except that if it is ugly the struggle over it will be more ironic. James, however, is not an ironist; no Puritan can be. And the fact that with this novel we can supply "real" tables and chairs from our own imagination makes *The Spoils of Poynton*, to my mind, more true to our common experience, hence more classic, than most of his fictions.

But that, for the moment, is beside the point. What I should like to bring out now is another peculiarity: that though James's people endlessly discuss and analyze, they never discuss the subjects that people in society usually do. Above all, politics. It is not true that well-bred people avoid talk of politics. They cannot stay away from it. Outrage over public events that menace, or threaten to menace, their property and privilege has devolved on them by birthright (though it can also be acquired), and they cannot help sharing it when more than two meet, even in the presence of outsiders, which in fact seems to act as a stimulant. This has surely been so from earliest times, and James's time was no exception, as we know from other sources. But from his fictions (forgetting *The Princess Casamassima*, where he mildly ventured into the arena), you could never guess that whispers—or shouts—ever burst out over the tea table regarding the need for a firm hand, for making an example of the ringleaders, what are things coming to, and so on. Dickens' Mr. Bounderby, although no gentleman, put the position in a nutshell with "The turtle soup and the gold spoon," his own blunt résumé of the trade unionist's unmistakable goals. As James's people are constantly telling each other how intelligent they are, more subtlety than this might be expected of them, but we can only hope it. What were Adam Verver's views on the great Free Trade debate, on woman suffrage, on child labor? We do not know. It is almost as if James wanted to protect his cherished creations from our knowledge of the banalities they would utter if he once let us overhear them speak freely.

Or let us try art. These people are traveled and worldly and often in a state of rapture over the museums and galleries they visit, the noble façades of mansions and dear quaint crockets of cathedrals. Yet they rarely come away from a morning of sightseeing with as much as a half-formed thought. They never dispute about what they have looked at, prefer one artist to another, hazard generalizations. In real life, they would certainly have had their ideas about the revolutions that were occurring in painting and sculpture. In Paris, if only out of curiosity, they would have rushed to see the Salon des Indépendants. Wild horses could not have kept them away. A bold pair, armed with a letter from Lady Sackville or Isabella Stewart Gardner, might have penetrated Rodin's studio. His bronze statue of Balzac in a dressing-gown, shown at the Salon des Beaux Arts, would already have led the travelers to take sides, some finding it disgusting and incomprehensible while others were calling it a "break-through." What would they have made of the nude Victor Hugo in plaster in the Luxembourg Garden? Or "The Kiss" ("Rather *too* suggestive"?) in marble? Unfailingly one would have heard judgments as to what was permissible and impermissible in art.

James himself, however unversed in politics he might have been, had no deficiency of art-appreciation. He wrote well and copiously about painting, sculpture, and architecture. But not in his novels. There all is allusion and murmurous, indistinct evocation of objects and vistas, in comparison with which Whistler's "Nocturne" is a sharp-edge photograph.

In the novels, a taboo is operating—a taboo that enjoins him, like Psyche in the myth or Pandora or Mother Eve, to steer clear of forbidden areas on pain of losing his god-sent gift. The areas on which neither he nor his characters may touch are defined by the proximity of thought to their surface—thought visible, almost palpable, in nuggets or globules readily picked up by the vulgar. Art in other hands might have been such an area, but James took the risk—after all, it was his own great interest—and he actually dared make it the ruling passion of several of his figures, at the price, however, of treating it always by indirection, as a motive but never as a topic in itself. If you think of Proust, you will see the difference.

With religion and philosophy, though, James is as circumspect as he is with politics. As son and brother, he must often have heard these subjects earnestly discussed, which perhaps accounts for his dislike of ideas in general. Or was this only a sense, which grew on him as he sought to find his own way, that he must not trespass on father's and brother's hunting preserve? In any case, with the exception of *The Bostonians*—a middle-period extravagant comedy, which he came almost to disavow, full of cranks, cults, emancipated women, do-gooders, religious charlatanry—neither he nor his characters has a word to say on these matters, nor—it should go without saying—on science. With so much of the stuff of ordinary social intercourse ruled out, the Jamesian people by and large are reduced to a single theme: each other. As beings not given to long silences, who are virtually never seen reading, not even a guidebook, that is what they are condemned to. Whenever a pair or a trio draws apart from the rest, it is to discuss and analyze and exclaim over an absent one—Milly or Maggie or Isabel. Yet here too there is a curious shortage of ideas of the kind you or I might formulate in discussing a friend. In their place are hints, soft wonderings, head-shakings, sentences hanging in the air; communication takes place between slow implication and swift inference: "Oh! Oh! Oh!" The word "Wonderful!" returns over and over as the best that can be said by way of a summing-up.

As James aged, his reticence or the reticence he imposed on his surrogates grew more "wonderful" indeed. With *The Wings of the Dove*, we arrive at a heroine of whom we know only three things: that she is rich, red-haired, and sick. She is clearly meant to be admirable, as we infer from the gasps and cries of the satellite figures around her—"Isn't she superb?," "Everything about you is a beauty," "beautiful," "a dove," "Oh you exquisite thing!" But vulgar particulars are never supplied. As James himself observed in his Preface, ". . . I go but a little way with the direct—that is with the straight exhibition of Milly; it resorts to relief, this process, whenever it can, to some kinder, some merciful indirection: all as if to approach her circuitously, deal with her at second hand, as an unspotted princess is ever dealt with. . . ." And he continues: "All of which proceeds, obviously, from her painter's tenderness of imagination about her, which reduces him to watching her, as it were, through the successive windows of other people's interest in her."

It is an extension of the method, of course, that worked so successfully in *The Spoils of Poynton*. There the "treasures" had only to be called by that name two or three times, the astonished words "rare," "precious," "splendid," to drop one by one from soft young lips, to convince the reader that "the nice old things" were worth squabbling over at least to those engaged in the squabble. But the moral splendor of a human being needs more demonstration than the museum quality of mobile property, at any rate in a novel. One can decide that the fuss being made about furniture is ridiculous or justified or a little of both, and, as I have been saying, it does not greatly matter which. It is unnecessary to fully sympathize with Mrs. Gereth's emotions to be amused by the lengths to which she will go in single combat, and in fact one senses James's own moral reserve on her subject. But the fuss made over Milly Theale makes one irritably ask why, what is so admirable about her that cannot be named, unless it is just her bank balance? Similar doubts may be felt about the Ververs, father and daughter, in *The Golden Bowl*.

Their creator's reluctance to furnish them with identifiable traits that might let us "place" them in real life has curious consequences for the principals of the late novels. These figures, one realizes, must be accepted on faith, as ectoplasms emanating from an entranced author at his desk, in short as ghostly abstractions, pale ideas, which explains, when you come to think of it, the fever of discussion they excite in the other characters. Those by comparison are solid. They have bodies and brains, however employed. Motives are allotted to them, such as plain curiosity (the Assinghams, Henrietta Stackpole) or money greed or sexual hunger (both seem to be working, though sometimes at cross-purposes, in Kate Croy, Morton Densher, Charlotte Stant), motives that give them a foot in the actual world. And if, despite their concerted effort of analysis, the principals they keep wondering over evade definition, if, unlike furniture, they cannot be established as universals standing for a whole class of singulars, Milly and Maggie and Chad remain nonetheless ideas of a sort. That is, ideas, expelled by a majestic butler at the front door, return by another entrance and stand waiting pathetically to be dressed in words.

Before leaving James, hoist—if I am right—by his own petard, I want to ask whether his exclusion of ideas in the sense of mental concepts was connected or not with the exclusion of common factuality. The two are not *necessarily* related. Consider Thomas Love Peacock. There the ordinary stuff of life is swept away to make room for abstract speculation. That, and just that, is the joke. It tickles our funny-bone to meet the denizens of *Nightmare Abbey*—young Scythrop, the heir of the house, and

Flosky, who has named his eldest son Emanuel after Kant, and Listless, up from London, complaining that Dante is growing fashionable. Each has his own bats in the belfry; there is a bad smell of midnight oil in the derelict medieval structure, where practical affairs are neglected for the necromancy of "synthetical reasoning." In hearty, plain-man style (which is partly a simulation), Peacock treats the brain's sickly products as the end-result of the general disease of modishness for which the remedy would be prolonged exposure to common, garden reality.

But for James, mental concepts, far from being opposed to the ordinariness of laundry lists and drains, seem themselves to have belonged to a lower category of inartistic objects, like the small article of "the commonest domestic use" manufactured by the Newsome family in *The Ambassadors*—I have always guessed that it was a brass safety-pin. But safety-pin or sink-stopper, it could not be mentioned in the text, any more than Milly Theale's cancer (if that is what it was), or, let us say, *The Origin of Species*. I confess I do not easily see what these tabooed subjects have in common, unless that they were familiar to most people and hence bore the traces of other handling. Yet, though both were in general circulation, a safety-pin is not the same as the idea of natural selection. More likely, James wished his fictions to dwell exclusively on the *piano nobile*, as he conceived it, of social intercourse—neither upstairs in the pent garrets of intel-lectual labor nor below in the basement and kitchens of domestic toil. And the **garret** and the basement have a secret sympathy between **them** of which the *piano nobile* is often unaware. That, at any rate, seems to be the lesson of the greatest fictions, past and present.

What is curious, though, is that ideas are still today felt to be unsightly in the novel, whereas the nether areas—the cloaca—are fully admitted to view. I suppose that the ban on ideas that even now largely prevails, above all in English-speaking countries, is a heritage from modernism in its prim anti-Victorian phase. To Virginia Woolf, for instance, it was not question of what might be brought *into* the novel—sex, the natural functions—but of what should be kept out. In the reaction against the Victorian novel, it was natural that the discursive authors, from Dickens to Meredith and Hardy, should stand in the pil-lory as warning examples of what was most to be avoided. When the young Eliot complimented James on the fact that no rough bundles of concepts disfigure and coarsen his novels, he at once went on to cite Meredith ("the disciple of Carlyle") as a bad case of the opposite.

Actually Meredith with his tendency to aphorism was in his own way an experimental writer, which made him exciting to the young. This may have been why he was singled out for rapid disposal. That he went counter to the "stuffy" realist tradition, jested with the time-honored conventions of the form, even gave hints of something like the interior monologue, did not excuse him. In fact he has not lasted, except, I think, for *The Egoist*; the mock-heroic vein, which he worked and overworked, failed to undermine the old structure and became a blind alley. Brio was not enough. In any case, his way with ideas, wavering between persiflage and orotund pronouncement, was too unsteady to maintain a serious weight. His contemporaries seem to have known what he was "about," but a reader today finds it hard to determine the overall pattern of his thought.

This can never be said of Dickens, George Eliot, Hardy. Nor on the Continent of Hugo, Stendhal, Balzac, even Flaubert, of Manzoni, or any of the Russians except Chekhov, who was relatively taciturn. The talkative, outspoken novelist was evidently the norm and always had been. In America, those who have survived—chiefly Melville and Hawthorne—seldom expressed themselves on topics and issues of the day, and their utterances could be somewhat riddling on the great themes of good and evil. Nevertheless they cannot be charged with unsteadiness, lack of serious purpose. They were sermonizers like their contemporaries in the Old World; it was only that their sermon, like the Book of Revelations, required some decoding; the apocalyptic imagery, as with an allegory, called for interpretation.

In fact the nineteenth-century novel was so evidently an idea-carrier that the component of overt thought in it must have been taken for granted by the reader as an ingredient as predictable as a leavening agent in bread. He came to expect it in his graver fiction, perhaps to count on it, just as he counted on the geographical and social coordinates that gave him his bearings in the opening chapter: the expanse of Egdon Heath at sundown crossed by the solitary reddleman and his cart; the mountain heights of the Lecco district looking down on the lone homeward-bound figure of Don Abbondio. Or "A rather pretty little chaise on springs, such as bachelors, half-pay officers, staff captains, landowners with about a hundred serfs . . . drive about in, rolled in at the gates of the hotel of the provincial town of N." Or "About thirty years ago, Miss Maria Ward, with only seven thousand pounds, had the good fortune to captivate Sir Thomas Bertram, of Mansfield Park, in the county of Northampton." We are so much in the habit of skipping pages of introductory description and general reflections that interrupt the story that we can scarcely believe that such "blemishes" once gave pleasure, that a novel would have been felt by our ancestors to be a far poorer thing without them. They can be dismissed by the modern reader as "mere" conventions of the genre, but in the old times a novel that lacked them would have been like an opera without an overture, which of course is a convention too.

The function of geographical descriptions—naming of counties, rivers, and so forth—and social topography is to make the reader feel comfortable in the vehicle he has boarded, like passengers in a plane having landmarks below pointed out to them and receiving bulletins from the pilot on altitude and cruising speed. Yet it was not essentially different from the function performed by ideas. Both gave depth and perspective. And the analogy to air travel is illustrative. The briefings supplied by the pilot ("On your left, folks, you'll see the city of Boston and the Charles River") are a relic of earlier days of aviation—a mere outworn convention we "put up with" in a contemporary airbus. Scarcely anybody bothers any more to rise in his seat to try to make out the landmark being mentioned—you cannot see anything anyway—the plane is going too fast and the view is obstructed. Besides, who cares? The destination is the point. But if you put yourself back in fancy to the propeller plane, you will see, as with the novel, what has been lost. So intrinsic to the novelistic medium were ideas and other forms of commentary, all tending to "set" the narration in a general scheme, that it would have been impossible in former days to speak of "the novel of ideas." It would have seemed to be a tautology.

Now the expression is used with such assurance and

frequency that I am surprised not to find it in my *Reader's Guide to Literary Terms*, which is otherwise reasonably current. For example, under "NOVEL," I read: "In the late nineteenth and twentieth centuries the novel, as an art form, has reached its fullest development. Concerned with their craft, novelists such as Flaubert, Henry James, Virginia Woolf, James Joyce, E. M. Forster, and Thomas Mann have used various devices to achieve new aesthetic forms within the genre." I do not know what Flaubert, who died in 1880, is doing there, but the tenor of the list is clear. If the "NOVEL OF IDEAS" does not figure as an entry (though "NOVEL OF THE SOIL" does), it may be that the authors were not sure what the term covered. I must say that it is not clear to me either, though I sense something derogatory in the usage, as if there were novels and novels of ideas and never the twain shall meet. But rather than attempt to define a term that has never been in my own vocabulary, I shall try to discover what other people mean by it.

Does it mean a novel in which the characters sit around, or pace up and down, enunciating and discussing ideas? Examples would be *The Magic Mountain, Point Counter Point*, in fact all of Huxley's novels, Sartre's *Les chemins de la liberté*, Malraux's *Man's Fate*. The purest cases would be Peacock—*Headlong Hall, Nightmare Abbey, Crotchet Castle*—if they could be called novels, which I doubt, since they lack a prime requisite—length —and another—involvement of the reader in the characters' fates. You might also count Flaubert's unfinished *Bouvard et Pecuchet*, where the joint heroes are busy compiling a Dictionary of Received Ideas, and Santayana's *The Last Puritan*, by now forgotten. But though the term would seem clearly to apply to the works just mentioned (*The Magic Mountain* being the one everybody remembers best, having read it at nineteen), there are not very many of them and they are rather out of style.

Solzhenitsyn's *Cancer Ward*, which belongs to our own time, roughly conforms to the type. Like *The Magic Mountain*, it takes place in a sanatorium, where patients who have come to be cured have little else to do after their treatments and medical examinations than muse and argue. Isolation is crucial to this type of novel: the characters are on an island, out on a limb, either of their own choosing—Peacock's crotchety castles, Huxley's grand country house presided over by Mr. Scogan (*Crome Yellow*)—or by force majeure, as in a hospital or a prison (Solzhenitsyn's *The Third Circle*). Or the island may be moral, self-constituted by a literary clique (*Point Counter Point*), by a group of like-thinking, semi-political Bohemians (*Les chemins de la liberté*), by a cell of revolutionaries (*Man's Fate*). What is involved is always a contest of faiths. The debates on the magic mountain between Naphta and Settembrini oppose nihilistic Jesuitry to progressive atheistic humanism but also pan-Germanism to pro-Russian *entente-cordiale* doctrine, prophecies of war to firm belief in peace, repose to work, in other words, you might say, night to day. Beneath the circus-like confrontation of current creeds lies a clash between very ancient faiths. Settembrini is a monist, Naphta a dualist. Settembrini, asked to choose, exalts mind over body: ". . . within the antithesis of body and mind, the body is the evil, the devilish principle, for the body is nature." It is like a game of preferences with the aim being self-definition, which no doubt is why young people are dazzled by it.

On a simpler level and without encyclopedic pretensions, *Cancer Ward* presents us with various naive faiths —from faith in Stalin to faith in the healing properties of radioactive gold to faith in the mandrake root—sometimes peacefully coexisting, sometimes at odds with each other. It is natural that in a hospital the belief in a cure, in sovereign remedies, should dominate every mind. It becomes vital to have a theory, and world theories, global diagnoses of the body politic or the human state generally, take on, as though of necessity, an importance not usually accorded them by the healthy. The pressing need to have faith, i.e., grounds for hope, gives an urgency to the abstract disputes of both *The Magic Mountain* and *Cancer Ward*. Here ideas of any and every kind become, as if by contagion, matters of life and death. It is also true that in these narratives no idea can win out over another. Nobody is convinced or persuaded. The excited debates between patients or between doctor and patient end up in the air. Hans Castorp, whose young mind has been the salient contested for by opposing forces, leaves the sanatorium and returns "down below," to the plains, which should be the level ground of sound, commonplace reality, except for the fact that there he dies as a soldier in the general reasonless catastrophe of the First World War. In *Cancer Ward*, Kostoglotov, too, leaves his sanatorium, having been let out as cured, which should be a happy ending, except for the fact that the cancer ward whose gates close behind him has been a species of sanctuary; he is slated to return to his real down-to-earth life of penal exile. One kind of death sentence, in both cases, has been exchanged for another.

It is not especially uncanny (or no more than any resemblance or twinning) that this pair of novels, so widely separated in space and time, so widely divergent in manner, should match in a number of respects. Sanatorium life is much the same, I suppose, everywhere and always. But sanatorium life, as such, did not dictate the ending; a positive conclusion would have been possible if the novel were only about sickness and recovery. The ending is imposed not by the particular case—cancer ward or tubercular clinic—but by the fact that in general the so-called novel of ideas (at least the kind I have been describing) does not allow of any resolution. Nothing decisive can happen in it; it is a seesaw. Events that do occur in it are simply incidents, sometimes diverting, as in Peacock. A real event, such as the death of Hans Castorp, is reserved for a postscript; it does not belong to the text proper. The same with Kostoglotov's re-shouldering of his penal identity. We do not see it happen; in fact it may not happen "for good," since when he goes to register with the NKVD in the town outside the hospital gates, the *Komendant* speaks cheerfully of an amnesty in the offing. But Kostoglotov cannot make himself believe him—he has heard of amnesties before and nothing came of them—and the reader knows no more than he. It is left in suspension, like the arguments between the sick men, which never "get" anywhere.

If a secondary character chances to die—for instance, Quarles' child in *Point Counter Point*—that, too, is an incident, outside the work's proper concerns; the main characters go on arguing as before. When it occurs in a sanatorium, it is just an episode, figuring in the normal mortality rate; a new patient moves into the bed the next day, and the ripple of concern quickly subsides. The sanatorium is an ideal setting for the discussion novel, for time does not count there. Ideas, though some may age, are indifferent to time. Mann speaks of "the more spacious time conceptions prevalent 'up here.' " That is an effect, of course, of the routine, which makes one day like another. But there is an endlessness, an eternal regularity, in all such novels; the characters slip into their places like habitués of a corner café. The sense of eternity may be represented under other aspects. In André Gide's *The Counterfeiters*, which I might have included under this heading, Edouard, the chief character, is shown writing a novel in which a facsimile of him is writing a novel, in which, we suppose, still a third figure . . . The black-hatted Quaker on the Quaker Oats box holding a Quaker Oats box portraying a Quaker holding a Quaker Oats box, getting smaller and smaller in infinite regress. In *Point Counter Point* Huxley borrowed the repeating-decimal device.

Still, when the novel of ideas is spoken of, maybe another type of story is being referred to—a story that does come to some sort of resolution. That is the missionary novel sometimes referred to as a "tract." On the surface it may look like the kind of novel I have just been trying to analyze, in that it may have the air of a panel discussion, with points of view put forward by several characters speaking in turn and each being allowed equal time. But it soon appears that one speaker is right and the others, though momentarily persuasive, are wrong. I am thinking of D. H. Lawrence.

Of course there are missionary novels that are not novels of ideas, for example, *Uncle Tom's Cabin*. It is animated by a strong conviction but, if I remember right, does not "go into" the argument for and against slavery. And there are missionary elements hiding in many tales that pass for thrillers or love stories. In fact it is hard to think of a novel that in some sense does not seek to proselytize. But what I have in mind are books like *Women in Love, Aaron's Rod, Kangaroo, Lady Chatterley's Lover*, where reasoning occupies a large part of the narrative, exerting a leverage that seems to compel the reader's agreement. The incidents, few or many, press home like gripping illustrations the point being proved. There is something of parable in most of Lawrence's plots.

In *Kangaroo* we get a powerful example of Lawrence's method at work. The ideas, fully expounded in long conversations, far from being unresolved, are boldly lived out and tested. The Lawrence figure, Somers, finds certain already held and seductive ideas made flesh for him in the shape of the Australian working-class leader known as Kangaroo. It is an incarnation Somers had never hoped to come upon, sickened as he is by Europe. He is smitten by Kangaroo's proto-fascist movement and by the wild fresh country of which working men and their virile matey principles seem to be a natural and harmonious part. The infatuation holds for many pages; he is drawn into the movement as a sympathetic foreign observer. He is nearly converted when, rather abruptly, he is startled into closer inspection: Kangaroo, dying, asks for a declaration of Somers' love, and the sickly plea lets Somers finally see the soft, weak, flabby underside of native fascism. The Australian spell is broken; Somers and his woman leave.

Up to the end, however, an equilibrium of ideas is maintained, so that the conversations remain interesting, by no means one-sided. In Somers, a genuine intellectual process, going from curiosity to attraction to repulsion and disillusionment, is shown with considerable honesty. It is typical of Lawrence at his best that even when Kangaroo and his ideas are rejected, he is not vulgarly "seen through"; something is left for a kind of dry pity and understanding.

Lady Chatterley's Lover is surely the most biased of Lawrence's books. Yet Sir Clifford, Lady Chatterley's husband, is nonetheless given his say, not too unfairly represented by and large; it is only that he and his entire set of convictions are refuted out of hand by a quiet adversary, Mellors, whose strong point is not words but *performance*. His performance is itself an argument, speaking for a view of natural life and sexuality that is hostile to the intellect. Sir Clifford is no intellectual; he is a retired country gentleman who sometimes writes poetry and short stories. But the weapons he is familiar with and falls back on as a disabled champion of a social order and mild way of life are the weapons his education has taught him to use: received notions and principles.

Lawrence's hatred of the intellect, of the "upper story" (there is maybe a class prejudice here), is strange, certainly, in a man who himself lived almost wholly for ideas. The fact that they were his own made the difference apparently; he had hammered them out for himself. They were not quite so much his own as he thought, one must add. Was he unconscious of being one of a number of writers who disliked and distrusted the intellect, who, like him, held it responsible for most of the ills of modern civilization? He showed no awareness of such a fellowship, just as he showed no awareness of a paradox underlying the whole position, that is, that without the intellect and its system-making bent neither he nor his fellow-thinkers would have been able to carry out their mission of teaching at all. His insistence on blood and instinct as superior to brain was a mental construct incapable of proof except on the mental level.

Yet if his ideas, true or false, have stayed with us, if he was a novelist of ideas in my second, missionary, sense to whom we can still listen—the only one, probably—this must be because he was an artist as well as a cogent, programmatic mind, in other words, because he makes us feel as we read those novels that there is *something* in what he says. But while despising the intellect, he would not have liked the name "artist" either. For him it would have been six of one and half a dozen of the other—who could measure which was the less effete? He was unable to get along with any of his own kind, really, and could only associate, finally, with people who shared his ideas, which was bound to mean in practice people who consented to have no ideas of their own.

His life was a near-tragedy, and his self-infection, quite early, with concepts—which, when he took them for absolutes, made him quarrelsome—shared responsibility with his bad lungs. But if he had not been fevered, he might not have taken to the stump, and we might never have had these burning novels or, if you wish, tracts. Far more than the discussion novels with their eternal seesaw, they are truly novels of ideas. Without ideas none of them, after *Sons and Lovers*, could even palely exist. If you cut out Naphta and Settembrini, and the author's musings on time, *The Magic Mountain* will still hold up as a story of a sort. The equivalent cannot be argued of *Aaron's Rod*, say. I am not sure whether this makes Lawrence better or worse than Mann; at any rate it makes him special. At the same time, surprisingly, it links him with the old novelists, to whom I shall turn next. If you are going to voice explicit ideas in a novel, evidently this requires a spokesman, and I shall begin by discussing the spokesman.

2

As I was saying, if you are going to voice ideas in a novel, plainly you will need a spokesman. In the traditional novel such semi-official figures are familiar to us and, on the whole, welcome. We quickly learn to recognize which of the characters will be a stand-in for the author, that is, which one we can trust as appointed representative with full powers to comment on what is happening and draw the necessary conclusions. There is nothing wrong with this; events in life seldom speak for themselves. Whether it is world events that confront us or local skulduggery— an ecological scandal or somebody running off with a friend's wife—we frequently want somebody to explain them to us, sketch in the background, suggest where our sympathies should lie. There is no reason we should be worse off in a novel, as long as the novel is assumed to have some reasonably close connection with our immediate life or a life we are acquainted with through reading and report.

The novel in its classic period—the nineteenth century —took on that burden without protest. Protest only began to be heard toward the end of the century, when the novel, aggrieved by how much it had been expected to carry on its increasingly slender shoulders, made the first motions toward emancipation. Up until James, the novelist had been a quite willing authority figure, a parent, aunt, in Tolstoy's case a Dutch uncle. The popular novelist (and there was no other kind, the art novel not having been discovered) was looked up to as an authority on all sorts of matters: medicine, religion, capital punishment, the right relation between the sexes. If the role was uncongenial or momentarily wearisome, he had the resort of the short story or the tale to turn to, neither of which carried such heavy responsibilities to the common life.

Lawrence was the last Westerner, probably, to accept the burden of being a universal authority, though there is some evidence of it in Norman Mailer. A clear sign, if one were needed, of Lawrence's willingness for the job is the presence of spokesmen—Rawdon Lilly, Somers, Birkin, Mellors—in his novels, and Mailer, too, has his mouthpieces. Lawrence makes an occasional, unconvincing attempt to disguise the spokesman or to split him into two.

In the nineteenth century there is no pretense of that sort; the author has not yet learned to be embarrassed by the device, which came to be regarded as crude, though in reality, as usually happens with cover-ups, the disguises are cruder.

In the classic novel, the spokesman may be the hero or heroine, but more rarely than became the custom later. In *Anna Karenina*, he is Levin, the name being pointedly derived from Tolstoy's own Christian name, Lev or Lyov. In *War and Peace*, there is no delegated spokesman; Pierre is too young and bumbling, and Prince Andrei is morally and spiritually too old, a case of *fin de race*— mention of his "small white hands" occurs too emphatically not to be a signal of disapproval. Instead, throughout *War and Peace*, Tolstoy speaks in his own voice: in the marvelous chapters on Napoleon, on the old fox, Kutuzov, on the battle of Borodino, on the multiple causes of wars; also in the terse parentheses concerning the uses of medicine, the mysterious undercurrents in the life of the Russian peasantry; finally in the Second Epilogue beginning "History is the life of nations and of humanity," which sets out in simple style the general conclusions on history, free will, and determinism a thoughtful reader will want to derive from all the events he has witnessed. The Second Epilogue is a kind of teaching instrument intended to sharpen the reader's understanding of the limits between the knowable and the unknowable. Tolstoy, as spokesman here, is uncompromisingly agnostic, except in the moral sphere: we have no way of inferring First Causes; we can only be sure about very small, almost minute, acts of our own, such as our freedom (assuming no physical impairment) to raise an arm in an empty room. Similarly, as readers, we can be sure that Natasha's going to the opera was the proximate cause of her moral fall; yet it is doubtful that she had any clear choice in the matter: a decision major in its consequences slipped by her without announcing itself as pregnant with causality.

When Tolstoy in *War and Peace* speaks to us of all these matters in his own voice, he is resorting to a method that goes back to the infancy of the novel, that of the omniscient narrator. His practice in *Anna Karenina*, published a bit later, was different, as we know. I doubt that to his mind this represented a technical advance; it seems likely that he used the method that appeared most suitable to the material he was going to treat. Odd as that sounds to us today, he regarded himself as a rebel against the tyranny of conventional forms, announcing in an afterword to *War and Peace* that the book was not a novel, even less a poem, still less a historical chronicle. It was "what the author wished and was able to express in the form in which it is expressed."

In eighteenth-century England, an author, e.g., Fielding, was commonly his own spokesman. A radical break in the tradition came with the epistolary novel, and this may explain the popularity of Richardson among the avantgarde of our own century. In the nineteenth century, practice varied. With George Eliot, there was a sort of division of labor. In *Middlemarch* she speaks now and again in her own deeply earnest voice, now and again through Dorothea Brooke, although with Dorothea it is less a matter of homiletic thought than of "right" feeling. George Eliot has another voice, though, quite different from her customary organ tones; it harks back to the eighteenth century and is dry, pungent, short-spoken, as when she suggests of Lydgate, not unsympathetically, that his otherwise fine character was "a little spotted with commonness." We have been advised by the curt phrase what to expect. The wonderful word "spotted," suggesting a case of measles—an ordinary, non-fatal disease—sticks, fatally for Mr. Lydgate, in the mind. She uses that third voice rather sparingly, but whenever it speaks, we hear judgment in it and are warned to pay attention.

In French nineteenth-century fiction, as one might expect, the division of labor between authors and characters was on the whole stricter. To the author speaking in his own voice was reserved the right of comment and general statement. Among the great luminaries jealous of place and prerogative, each a *roi soleil* outshining his *dramatis personae*, pre-eminence in this respect as in others goes to Victor Hugo. That god-like seer, mage, and prophet could not delegate authority to any of his mortals. The self-educated Jean Valjean, the poor babes Marius and Cosette, *le petit Gavroche*—street urchin playing Mercury—all those *misérables* who make up the wronged part of humanity must be spoken *for* by an advocate, standing protectively between them and us. You have something very similar in Manzoni, though with less pomp and circumstance: a kind of tender paternalism toward the humble—Lucia and Renzo but also the wretched parish priest, Don Abbondio.

It is surprising to notice how rarely Hugo allows us to enter the mind of Jean Valjean, even for the sake of glimpsing his state of feeling at a given moment. The emotions there are inferred for us by Victor Hugo and reported in summary form. This applies to the whole cast of characters. For instance, rather early in the book there is an examination of capital punishment and the feelings it produces in the spectator. Bishop Myriel, we are told, has been obliged in his younger days to witness an execution, and it has brought about a great change in his outlook. Another author would have shown us that reaction and those reflections through the old Bishop's consciousness as it remembers, but Hugo describes the whole ex-

perience in his own terms, reconstructing it like an archae-
ologist's sketch from fragments he feels must be buried
in Myriel's memory. He summarizes *on behalf of* the
Bishop. In fact he almost never claims to enter the consciousness of any of his creatures. He speculates on what
may be there and has recourse to metaphor and analogy to
convey it, as in the entire short chapter in which Jean
Valjean's state of mind is evoked by the image of a drown-
ing man abandoned by the ship of civilization. Similarly
with the Bishop's faith, an important force in the book;
we see it at work, like the effect of wind on grass, but we
do not penetrate into its inner make-up or constitution,
any more than one would try to get inside a wind. It is no
different with the bad people in the book. He guesses what
must be passing through the mind of Javert in the scene
with Fantine in the police-station, just as he guesses at the
reasons for Jean Valjean's growing love for the little or-
phaned Cosette: wasn't it, perhaps, that the convict's soul
was in need of revictualing in order to persevere in the
good?

Some of this, of course, is simply a device—an old novelist's trick—to make us accept the pretense that the story
is real, that it has an existence independent of its author,
who is as much in the dark as the rest of us as to what is
going on inside these people. But something more than
make-believe is involved here for Victor Hugo. There is a

delicacy of feeling in the decision to stay *outside*. It is as though the mind of another—even a fictional other—were a private room, whose threshold ought not to be crossed by anyone but the occupant. A mind, no matter whose, is a *hortus conclusus*, like the immaculate maiden's chamber with potted lily and prayer books which only the Angel Gabriel is allowed to invade. Hugo is a chaste novelist, respecting the chastity of his characters. The inside of the dread Javert, as much as that of the saintly Bishop, remained *virgo intacta*.

The exceptions to the rule are significant. Twice in *Les Misérables* he lets us see a process of reasoning that is going on in Jean Valjean's head. On the first occasion he is struggling within himself as to whether he shall give up his new respectable identity—which shelters a new self—to save a man falsely accused of being the escaped convict Jean Valjean. It is a struggle between two kinds of duty: duty to his new, actively virtuous and altruistic self, which he fears he will lose by avowing who he is, and duty to a single other person. The inner argument is long; there are equally convincing, equally high-minded arguments in favor of either course. In the end, as you know, he appears dramatically in the courtroom and declares who he is.

The second time, hundreds of pages later, that we are allowed access to his soul or brain, he is once more locked in a struggle. It is after Cosette's marriage, and the question facing him in his long-maintained third identity as Monsieur Fauchelevent is whether he shall share the happiness of the young couple, as they wish him to do, "bring his dark destiny into their bright foyer" or quietly go away. As he says, sharing their happiness will require his perpetual silence about the grim facts of his history, his continuing to live a lie, which has been justified by the necessity of being a father to Cosette but is so no longer. Again the inner argument is long, many valid points are to be made on both sides, and again it ends in a decision to avow who he is, this time to Marius, Cosette's husband. It is clear, I think, why in these two, special cases, Victor Hugo lets us hear what is going on in Jean Valjean's *for intérieur*, that is, his conscience, or inner tribunal. What we are overhearing in both cases is a *dialogue*. There are always two voices in a conscience, both usually claiming to be the voice of duty, and Jean Valjean is reasoning with himself, almost as if he were speaking aloud.

In these two interior dialogues lies the heart of the book, which is a story of pursuit. Jean Valjean's bodily pursuer is Inspector Javert, who can be evaded and finally done away with; his moral pursuer is the truth, which hunts him down in his last retreat, his conscience, where after many vicissitudes he had good reason to believe himself safe.

That is the Idea of the novel. As Hugo himself formulates it in a characteristic passage, "A man's conscience is that bit of infinity he harbors in himself and against which he measures the volitions of his brain and the acts of his life." I say "characteristic" because there we find Hugo performing the big task he imposed on himself of giving a wider view than his *misérables* are capable of having, placed where they are, near the bottom of society. The Idea of the story has been lived by Jean Valjean; he has wrestled with it and borne it on his strong shoulders like the weight of Marius that he carried through the sewers of Paris. But he would be unable to express it.

From time to time, Hugo evidently felt the need to state magisterially how the book should be understood. For example, toward the beginning of the second volume, "This book is a drama whose chief character is the infinite. Man is the second." At the beginning of Volume Three, he tells us that the novelist is "the historian of morals and ideas," which implies a rather different stance, one of non-involvement. And it is true that in this volume, which deals with the 1839 events, he reports on the one hand the ideas of Marius, originally conservative, and on the other those of the embattled young men of the secret societies who will lead the May rising and man the barricades. In the manner of Caesar, he even gives us their pre-battle harangues. It is plain, moreover, that their ideas are being recorded by the author as historian, that they are not his own. Though he shows sympathy for the ardor and courage of an Enjolras, he himself was a believer in Progress. That in fact is the final explanation he offers of the underlying meaning of his novel (Volume Three, page 269): "The real title of this drama is: Progress."

Actually this assertion is far from borne out by the novel itself, whose real title is its real title: *les Misérables*. The pursuit theme, illustrated in the smallest cruel particulars of keyhole spying and motiveless delation, points to the hopelessness of trying to throw off the dead hand of the past. However much we reform our ways, grow a new self, we *are* our past; it lurks behind us, follows us, denounces us, tracks us down. The novel ends with the utter isolation of Jean Valjean. You could say that social advance, an enlightened rehabilitation program for convicted offenders, would have remedied that. But that is not what the story says. By an immense solitary effort Jean Valjean had been able to change. He *is* a new man, but the new man, at the moment of promised happiness, only encounters a new pursuer, sterner than Javert: "To be happy we must never understand what duty is; once we understand it, it is implacable." None of this resembles progressive doctrine.

Still, it must have been Hugo's asserted faith in the

deity of Progress—always written with a capital, like God's name—that let him record without palliation the unhappiness, the mass misery, of the nation. And it was the wretched not of the earth but of France that weighed so heavy on him. How would he have been able to write of their suffering unless at the same time he had been able to offer the reader—and perhaps, above all, himself—the consolation of belief in a gradual improvement through the movement of History? His belief in historical progress was inseparable from his belief in France as the appointed successor to Greece and Rome in the sacred role of leader of nations. *"La révolution française est un geste de Dieu,"* he shouts in fierce italics, as if defying any contradiction. The manifest destiny of France to lead and inspire was identified by Hugo with his own mission to the nation as seer and epic novelist.

Hence the hymns to Progress issuing as if from the choir loft to temper the lesson of barbarity, greed, and fatuous ignorance being read and absorbed below. Hence also that passion for instruction, for the imparting of factual knowledge that impels him, for instance, to write twenty-two pages on *argot*, the pretext being the introduction of the street *môme*, Gavroche. The descent of Jean Valjean into the Parisian sewer system excuses a four-page essay called "The Intestine of Leviathan," which is full of information and meritorious ideas, for example on the advantages for the municipality of using human excrement as fertilizer—an anticipation of today's ecological thinking that unfortunately still remains "only" an idea. Hugo was an extremely intelligent and far-sighted man, and to know this of himself was to feel the duty of sharing. He has an obligation, fired by public spirit, to tell us the history of the Bernardine Order of nuns (Cosette is being harbored in the convent), to explain which Parisian cemeteries are disaffected and which are still in use (Jean Valjean, alias Monsieur Fauchelevent, is about to be buried alive), even to leap ahead to analyze the revolution of 1848, which took place nine years *after* the events we are reading about.

His ambition to get everything in, to make this book *the* Book, reflected a kind of evangelical zeal which he had in common with most of the serious novelists of his century. One thinks of Balzac's excursus on the paper industry (*Les illusions perdues*), of Tolstoy on Pierre's Freemasonry, of Dostoievsky on the Russian monk, of Manzoni on St. Charles Borromeo and on the daily mortality figures of the great plague of 1630 in Milan. Melville on whaling or George Eliot on the discoveries of Bichat in the field of medical pathology. For our own century, we may think of Proust on Venice, on Vermeer, on the newly introduced telephone system, but more emphatically, perhaps, of Joyce in *Finnegans Wake*, which he, too, aspired to make *the* Book embracing the whole of human history and its tongues in a perfect spiralling form. Though public spirit as an animating force was no longer evident (in fact the reverse) in either Joyce or Proust, the ambition to produce a single compendious sacred writing survived, and we may even find it today in an author like Pynchon (*Gravity's Rainbow*).

Of course not all novels were so informative; one reminds oneself of Jane Austen, who is to the novel as Wordsworth's *Lyrical Ballads* were to *The Prelude*. One must remember, too, that the novel of travel and exploration was a popular species by itself catering to a growing thirst for information: Marryat, Melville, Pierre Loti, Conrad were sailor novelists—a new literary type. Some of these tended toward the encyclopedic (*Moby Dick*), while the fictions of Conrad, on the other hand, went so far in the direction of brevity and concentration that they were closer to the tale than to the novel. Yet the element of vouched-for authenticity that seemed to be demanded of the sea story (no doubt because of the marvels of the deep it reported, like the Ancient Mariner, to those who stayed home) brought it close to the memoir, to such a piece of autobiography as Richard Henry Dana's *Two Years Before the Mast*. Typically, the line between Melville's *Typee* (fact) and his *Omoo* (fiction) is hard to perceive. With scientific advances, the factual and the fabulous seemed to draw together and each to guarantee the other—stranger than fiction. *The Voyage of the Beagle* was a kind of adventure story. Waterways and landways "opened up" fresh territory, and geography, more and more, as with Huck Finn's raft and Kurtz's up-river station, was understood as a metaphor for the dark continent of the human heart. At the same time, like the *National Geographic*, this literature was *educational. Kim*, a best-seller, was boy's book, romance, *Bildungsroman*, and dry-as-dust dispenser of ethnographical lore.

In other words, fictions, including the novel, were meeting a new need created by the fact that the horizon had vastly extended while the means of conveying information had not developed to keep pace. The newspapers were unequipped for the job of reporting on distant events and discoveries—the telegraph was just being invented. Photography was still in its early days, which made the "word pictures" of the novelist—themselves a rather recent invention—an enormous public service. In the absence of radio, films, television, news magazines, the novel kept the public in touch with what was happening in science, manufacturing, agriculture, and so on. Indeed it sometimes seemed to accept the functions of a mail-order catalogue or a farmer's almanac, as in *Tess of the D'Urbervilles* when the bright-blue new turnip-slicing machine and the still newer bright-red thresher are introduced to the farm laborers. The novel was not only a conveyor of factual information. It filled the place of today's round tables and seminars that people watch on television or listen to on the radio and that is the commonest source of their general ideas.

In any case, the immense fullness of Victor Hugo (which leads many to fear, mistakenly, that he is unreadable) was not a peculiar deformity, not a species of giantism resulting from a swollen ego. In France, you have it in Balzac, whose title *The Human Comedy* declares the resolve to encompass the entire species. And Balzac, like Hugo, remained his own spokesman, undisputed lord of his creation. But there is a marked difference in manner and tone. Hugo's assumption of the mantle of advocate for his *misérables* rested on compassion. His determination to widen the view, to soar above his narrative, implied no detachment of feeling. But Balzac was detached, to the point of being unsympathetic, often, with his principal figures, most noticeably in that strange masterpiece *Les illusions perdues*. Lucien de Rubempré (whose real name is Chardon like the lowly thistle) is a pathetic example of *l'esprit du siècle*. That is, he is an *arriviste*, endowed with two gifts—beauty and literary talent—on which he intends to capitalize. We are never allowed to know how much talent he really has—no samples are given of his historical novel, *The Archer of Charles IX*—

but his worldly career is an abject fizzle. He lays siege to Paris, scales its heights briefly, is repulsed with humiliating rapidity, driven back to his province, where he has brought ruin not only on himself but also on his devoted sister and brother-in-law, who have "believed" in him. What they have believed in is not the frail creature they knew too well but the idea of "genius" incarnate in him like a promise that cannot be broken.

The spirit of the age, then, is one of rapacious opportunism. Many examples are held up for almost loving inspection. Monstrous specimens from the big pond of Parisian literary life compete in gross rascality with the entrepreneurs and small lawyers of the provincial backwater, and the only distinction, doubtless not foreseen by Balzac, is that the shamelessness of Parisian literary circles is probably more believable than before—that depraved milieu has not changed with time but only become more itself, like an essence or concentrate. Balzac lets us see that a few rare innocents are to be found both in dull, dead Angoulême and the capital; in the provinces one might expect that they would be slightly more numerous, but it is not so. Lucien himself is a false innocent; he fails because he is a *weak* opportunist. His utter lack of self-knowledge may have at the beginning a naive, ingenuous charm but it is soon revealed as simple cowardice: he does not want to have a clear picture of the base actions he is about to commit that will then "add up to" a self he does not wish to know. It would be wrong to say that he is satirized; he is far too weak for that. It takes a more robust figure, like Meredith's Sir Willoughby Patterne (also utterly lacking in self-knowledge), to stand up to satire. Lucien hovers on the verge of being a comic figure, as he hovers on the verge of the literary world. Toward the end, he has decided or, rather, *thinks* he has decided to commit suicide—the only manly act left for him after the wrong he has done his family. Then, on reflection: *"J'ai toujours le temps de me tuer"* ("I've always got time to kill myself"). So instead he accepts a cigar.

It would be hard for Balzac to sympathize greatly with Lucien. He is too much an embodiment of the century, seeming to start out well, endowed with that lauded "genius" and with a *"beauté surhumaine,"* and then turning shallow and self-seeking, like France after 1815, which, for Balzac (and for Stendhal and Flaubert, too), had been converted into a nation of calculating machines. *Les illusions* is a critique of the age, of most of its ideas and motives, though, as if to compensate, the author gives us a swift, approving sketch of a group of poor young provincials in Paris that he calls the Cénacle—all selfless men of principle, including a European federalist. And with the figure of David Séchard, the printer who becomes Lucien's brother-in-law, he is directing the reader's attention to where the true genius of the century may lie: David is an inventor. His fatal, innocent error is to suppose that Lucien's lofty gift is superior to his own modest one: as his inferior, he feels himself bound to "stake" Lucien to a career in the capital, at the cost of doing without in his own domestic life, and, ultimately, of signing away *his* future (the patent), losing his once-thriving printing business, and being imprisoned for debt. Lucien, in fact, is his evil genius; surely the play on words was in Balzac's mind and was meant to come into the reader's.

Les illusions perdues, without question, is a novel ruled by ideas, just as its chief characters are. Even David Séchard, it is said, "will be the Jacquard of the paper industry"—Jacquard, the inventor of the improved loom, revolutionized the textile industry, and in this self-inflating Balzacian world, an invention, like a literary work, cannot simply make a contribution; it must be revolutionary and upset the prevailing order of things. Balzac is the great spokesman for the idea-driven slaves of concepts, yet (unlike Victor Hugo) he rarely expresses himself in conceptual terms. That is left to his men of letters, who in dialogue—or, more often, monologue—have the habit of writing critical essays aloud, like Sorbonne lecturers addressing an amphitheatre, though their auditory here consists only of Lucien. Along with the astonished Lucien, we learn, for example, the distinction between *la littéra-*

ture idéée and *la littérature imagée,* which in practical language is the difference between Voltaire and Walter Scott. Balzac himself (as we know from other sources) had toyed with such a distinction, and this must mean that he regarded it at least half-seriously. But when in *Les illusions* we hear it expounded by a literary journalist and master charlatan, the effect is one of parody. In other words, Balzac, in assigning a fond idea of his own to a fictional character who is decidedly *not* himself, has marked a distance separating him from his character. His detachment is, if anything, underlined: that nice distinction, his brain child, was now an orphan, joining all the other ideas à la mode that were floating about the literary world, the flotsam of raw data that will be blended into the story. *"Littérature idéée, littérature imagée,* that's how they talked, the reviewers. Remember?"

When he does speak in his own voice, Balzac usually limits himself to a kind of factual instructiveness that widens the picture but certainly does not ennoble it. Indeed, the aim appears to be precisely the contrary: to make what is already prose more prosaic by letting the reader see the processes at work behind the façade. A social mechanism or group of mechanisms—say the distribution of first-night theatre tickets to influential persons—is explained, just as in a guided visit to an industrial plant. In this volume the production and reception of literary works, including stage plays, is the theme, and everything is seen in terms of a giant economic process, in which reviewers, publishers, booksellers, actresses, authors are as much a part of the machinery as the paper mill or printing press. We learn how advertising revolutionized the book trade, how the *affiches* in shop windows and boulevard displays, which were the earliest examples of book advertising, were replaced by ads in newspapers and how this did away with the immense power of critics' notices and the dependence of publishers on journalists. And we learn a great deal, naturally, about the manufacture of paper and the history of printing processes, as well as many other interesting things, such as the difference between country attorneys and Parisian attorneys and how that affects the jailing of a man for debt.

All this, of course, has a bearing on the story, and I do not know whether a present-day novelist, deprived of the right of auctorial intervention, could succeed in telling such a complicated story at all.

With Stendhal, the spokesman's role is divided. In *The Red and the Black*, Stendhal speaks sometimes *through* Julien, sometimes on *behalf* of him, and sometimes *about* him. Julien, who has acute self-knowledge, is a far more intense and demanding center of interest for his creator than Victor Hugo's and Balzac's heroes were for them.

Yet this stops short of complete identification. Stendhal and Julien are two separate people, which would not be the case today. Occasionally he leaves Julien and the other characters entirely behind, as in the long parenthesis containing the famous statement "A novel is a mirror on the highway." This abrupt interruption of his own narrative is addressed to an imaginary reader: *"Eh, monsieur, un roman est un miroir qui se promène sur une grande route."* But there are other interjections, less programmatic and that do not have parentheses around them, though in reality they are "asides," as in a theatre. While noting the chronic dissatisfaction of Mathilde de la Mole, who "has everything," he remarks that in the convent she had been given the idea that because of her advantages of birth and wealth she should be happier than the others; then he suddenly reflects: "Here is the source of the boredom and follies of princes—an idea that has been planted in them." The aside could belong to La Rochefoucauld or even Montaigne. Sometimes the aside may be almost imperceptible as author's commentary and yet have a whole ethos compressed in it. Of the old curé of the town of Verrières: "despite his age . . . his eyes sparkled with the sacred fire that betrays the pleasure anticipated in doing a beautiful and slightly dangerous action." The play between asides and narrative, the contrast in texture among Julien's own thoughts—often identical, one

51

would guess, with Stendhal's own (*"En vérité, l'homme a deux êtres en lui, pensa-t-il"*) and often naively divergent from what a grown man would think—give the novel a shot-silk or quicksilver quality, an elusiveness of final commitment that is typical of Julien himself despite his iron resolves. The poles of heart and head—the first being Mme de Rênal, the second Mathilde—exercise an alternating attraction-repulsion on Julien, and of course they are *in* Julien, who switches from heart to head in the course of a single hour. He prefers Mme de Rênal, just as he prefers the impulses of his heart when he is lucky enough to feel them to the calculations of his head, but it is the black—the head, if the heart is the red—that governs. One cannot help reading it as an irony that this youth wholly directed by his will should die on the scaffold for a temporary aberration that led him, when beside himself, to commit a *crime passionnel.*

Julien's course, from the moment we meet him, is determined by ideas. In this he is different from Fabrizio in *The Charterhouse of Parma* and less attractive. He is programmed, like a just-invented computer, by an idea of duty *to himself.* That idea—not inclination—compels him to touch Mme de Rênal's hand for the first time and retain it in his grasp when she seeks to draw it away; soon he owes it to himself as the logical next stage to enter her bedroom and possess her. The same strict duty prevails in his relations with Mlle de la Mole, and always he is surprised by his failure to feel the appropriate emotions—the emotions he has learned from books that he *ought* to feel. As his tenseness gradually relaxes with Mme de Rênal, he does, to his joy, experience something recognizable to him as passion, even a devotion of the body in which his mind is not involved. This cannot happen with Mathilde de la Mole, who is too much like him. She too has been led, or misled, by books: *Manon Lescaut, La Nouvelle Héloïse, Letters of a Portuguese Nun.* Having imbibed Voltaire as well as amorous literature, she has hopes for Julien as a "new Danton." Each is imitating an accepted model—an idea—of passionate love, with disappointing results. Noting his lack of happiness during their first tryst, Julien has recourse to reason, which tells him he *should* be happy, *listing* the reasons. As if to prime the pump, he has just recited some sentences from *La Nouvelle Héloïse* to her.

The discrepancy between actual feeling and expected feeling is a leading motif here as in most of Stendhal. One of Julien's social assets is a prodigious memory; he first makes his mark at the seminary in Besançon by being able to recite any passage from the Bible on demand. But to know it by heart when he has not taken it *to* heart is a monstrosity. He has not a trace of religion in him. Careful observation has pointed to the church as the sole career open to his talents, and the disparity of pious outside and impious inside gives him, in his eternal black, the aspect of a hypocrite. That, in the end, is the charge he levels against himself in the solitude of his prison cell, and he is ready to go to the scaffold to refute it. His duty to some kind of consistency in himself forbids him to make use of Mathilde's ultra-ist connections and petition the detested crown for mercy.

Like Lucien de Rubempré, born Chardon, Julien is a parvenu. Or—the English word sits on him better—an upstart. And Stendhal is able to feel a half-tender admiration for him as an entirely self-made product. There is pardon, moreover, for Julien given, as it were, in advance of sin, in the picture Stendhal draws of the milieu—a duly objective picture that demonstrates that ambition and calculation are not so unnatural here as they might appear. Taken around the town of Verrières, we see the brutal necessity compelling him to which Julien has conformed his own will. He is self-made, but the tools his will had to work with were of Verrières manufacture.

Born under-privileged, the son of a sawmill operator ("the carpenter's son" is a gibe he hears too often on his upward-mobile course), delicate, pale, slender, hated by father and brothers, he likes to fancy himself as a foundling. His bookishness and mental gifts make him an object of general suspicion and enforce him in his sense of isolation. He is an idea in his own mind seeking recognition and repelling it with ferocity when he meets it. His poverty and low birth have made him proud, exacting, and distrustful. An insane pride is his undoing, and this insanity, which goes along with his ambition and at the same time constantly thwarts it, is what Stendhal respects in him. Julien is too proud to serve and too proud, finally, even to be self-serving like the common trucklers of his time. His duty to himself contains a higher duty, to the self as pure principled idea.

I have often thought that in plotting the steps of Julien's career Stendhal intended a wicked analogy with the career of Jesus. The "son of a carpenter," sure that his nominal "father" cannot be his real father, who, socially speaking, is on high (the notion of being the by-blow of a nobleman gradually gains hold of Julien's mind), our hero has his John the Baptist in his only friend, Fouqué, with whom early in his career he sojourns in the wilderness, at Fouqué's little sawmill up the River Doubs— Jordan. Like Jesus, Julien is surrounded by faithful women—Mathilde and Mme de Rênal, two sorrowing Marys; he is crucified (the guillotine) and buried. Mathilde and the loyal Fouqué accompany his body to the tomb, a grotto of Julien's own choosing high in the Jura mountains which Mathilde in due course will have embellished, like an early-Christian basilica, with Italian marble sculptures. Meanwhile, in the grotto "magnificently illuminated by an infinite number of tapers," the last rites are sung by twenty priests, and all the inhabitants of the little mountain villages, attracted by the strange ceremony, have followed the cortège. Christ's burial and apotheosis seem to have telescoped.

Well, there is no way of proving it or disproving it. Stendhal was given to mystifications, and this little blasphemy may have been one of them. If so, it would have been a shaft of mockery aimed at the century with the following message attached: if Christ were reborn in our debased and hypocritical time, He would come, as befits the age, in the shape of the upstart Sorel, and you would send Him to the guillotine, monsieur. . . .

The Red and the Black is not the only novel that illustrates the evil effects of reading. There is quite a string of them, going back to *Don Quixote*, whose hero's initial error sprang from reading chivalrous romances. These tales of chivalry unhinged him, so that he mistook the age he was living in, took prosaic windmills for castles, a peasant wench for a lady, and a broken-down jade for a charger. An idea had been implanted in him that rough reality, however often encountered, was powerless to correct. That Don Quixote, though mad, is a hero he owes to the fact that, like Julien Sorel, he remains true to his fixed idea. Catherine Morland in *Northanger Abbey* is in a similar case except that the Gothic romances she has stuffed herself with have made her fearful rather than brave; in an everyday world with its own perils, she is a prey to Gothic terror. She is the weakest, in both senses, of Jane Austen's heroines, perhaps because her mistakes do not originate in her distinct self, as Emma's do or even Anne's (Anne is persuadable by nature), but are traceable to outside influences—bad literature—like a common cold she has caught.

In *Nightmare Abbey* Peacock's characters have been completely vitiated by reading—*Werther*, Kant, Dante's *Purgatorio*, Burke on the Sublime ("A conspiracy against cheerfulness"), stronger stuff than Catherine Morland was exposed to, and the effect is more lasting. In Meredith's *The Egoist*—Meredith for a time was Peacock's son-in-law—Sir Willoughby Patterne's dreadful habit of discoursing with himself inside his head is said to be the result of reading "imaginative compositions of his time," i.e., popular romances. And on the other hand there is the wise youth Adrian of *The Ordeal of Richard Feverel*, who "had no intimates except Gibbon and Horace," but the consequences for *his* moral fiber, which is prematurely wizened and shrunken, seem to be even more deplorable. This "epicurean," who is always quoting a cynical poet called "Sandoe"—an author of Meredith's own invention—is a curious yet fitting associate for poor Sir Austin Feverel in his System for educating young Richard.

Emma Bovary's ruin can be seen to have its origin in the books she read in the convent and on her father's farm—books that "put ideas" in her head. The incriminated texts were not just cheap romances; she read Chateaubriand and George Sand, as well as Eugène Sue. Monsieur Homais, too, was a reader. We are not given his book list, but an article he has read in some journal is the source of his addled, sinister project to have Charles Bovary operate on Hippolyte's clubfoot. The only benign and harmless people in that novel are Charles, who cannot stay awake over a book, and non-readers like the illiterate servant-girl Félicité.

D. H. Lawrence comes to mind again, though I do not remember any citations of specifically harmful reading matter mentioned by him. But I can supply, finally, a quite recent example from a living author. Solzhenitsyn in *August 1914* lays the disastrous defeat on the Eastern Front that culminated in the battle of Tannenberg in part if not wholly at the door of the Russian generals who had read *War and Peace*. These high-placed fools, he tells us, were seeking to imitate the strategy of Kutuzov as described in the novel—a strategy, or tactic, of delay and evasion that was totally out of place in the circumstances of the Masurian Lakes campaign of the First World War and in any case, according to Solzhenitsyn, had been "romanced" by Tolstoy with no support from historical fact. The quite unnecessary (as he sees it) collapse at Tannenberg, ending in the suicide of General Samsonov, demoralized the Czarist Army and thus paved the way for the general debacle of 1917, which led to the Bolshevik seizure of power. Hence the popularity of *War and Peace* was a large contributing factor in the creation of the Soviet state.

It is natural for the common man in an irritable mood to pronounce on the dangers of reading novels. What is strange is to hear this from novelists, among them some of the greatest: Cervantes, Jane Austen, Stendhal, Flaubert. Of course the tone varies. With Jane Austen there is a teasing playfulness in the indictment, while for Flaubert the circulating library and its patrons are a source of pure disgust. For him, the spread of the plague of literacy to which the *cabinet de lecture* can be traced belongs among contemporary evils that are probably incurable. The multiplication of readers, like the mass production of cacti and oleographs, is a tedious illustration of the typically bourgeois phenomenon of repetition, adding to the universal sameness and satiety.

If the circulating library in Rouen had only nourishing books to lend culture-hungry Emma Bovary, the social effect would be even more depressing. A bad book is not harmed by circulating among the populace, but a superior one is brought down to the general level. This will be the fate of *Madame Bovary*; Flaubert has no illusions about raising subscribers to his own level—the iron law will not be suspended in his case. The fault is not even with future Emma Bovarys who will be tempted by Emma's example and devour the novel for "the wrong reasons," thus reducing it by a natural and inevitable process to *merde*. The fault is in "the art of the novel" itself, which copies life, which copies art, so that there is no end to the vulgarity of it. The labor of composition, the search for the *mot juste*, betray the novelist as grubby imitator toiling for a pointless exactitude. All forms of art, obviously, are open to that suspicion, but in the others—music, theatre, painting, sculpture—there is an element of play, of making (*poiēsis*), or just making believe. Even the sister art of poetry is allied to performance, i.e., to the alive; it may be declaimed or recited and in Flaubert's time often was. But, for both writer and reader, the novel is a lonely, physically inactive affair. Only the imagination races, and, in the case of the writer, disgust is quick to supervene. How cold and dead the words are, lying unresponsive on the page.

That there is something repellent to the practitioner himself in the practice of novel-writing may have to do with the servility of the form and with the fact that so little bodily action enters into it. The poet walks about and, as we know from Nadezhda Mandelstam, his lips move. Flaubert, if I remember right, did occasionally bawl out his sentences as he composed them, and other novelists of his day (e.g., George Eliot) wept while writing their "big" climactic scenes. Their tears were matched by their readers'; grown men cried over novels then. In fact the writer's shedding of tears—no longer admissible today—revealed the novelist as split into two, susceptible reader and methodically calculating author, conscious of his "craft." The tears were perhaps his penance for being the unmoved mover of masses. If the novel almost from its inception seems to be divided against itself, can this be because of its capacity for moving large numbers of people to extreme states of horror, suspense, longing, apprehension, while engineering no catharsis?

Stated in the simplest terms, the novelist's complaint against the novel is that it over-stimulates the reader, puts ideas in his head. It seems to me, looking back over what I have said, that in the past atonement for this was twofold. First, that the novelist be emotionally affected to the highest degree himself (those shouts and tears; Dickens' dramatic readings from his works, particularly Little Nell's death, the strain of which was thought to have brought on his own), and, second, that the novel, aware

61

of its dangerous propensity, should compensate by factual exposition and moral instruction. Just as the biographies of so many of the great novelists bear awful witness to the agonies their writings caused them (how often, like George Eliot, like Flaubert, like Lawrence, Proust, Joyce, Virginia Woolf, the novelist was a human sacrifice to his "heroic" creativity), so the intellectual and expository component in the novels of the great period was immense. The ratio was far larger than that in the drama and matched only, at moments, by that in the long narrative poem, say, "The Excursion" or *The Scholar-Gipsy*.

When, with James, the novel renounced its actuality, renounced its power to move masses—in short, its vulgarity in both senses of the word—it no longer had any need for ideas to undo the damage that verisimilitude and a high emotional involvement might do the reader tensely following its episodes. That sort of damage, genuine or imagined, could never have been caused by the theatre even at its most weepy and melodramatic, because the theatre is a public, forum-like art and its audience is not a collection of solitudes sitting in rows side by side. It was not until the invention of the moving-picture that the novel lost its supremacy as purveyor of irreality to a multitude composed of solitary units. In certain scenes (I think) of *Middlemarch* and *Nostromo*, the approach of the silent film can already be felt.

But, unlike the novel, the moving-picture, at least in my belief, cannot be an idea-spreader; its images are too enigmatic, e.g., Eisenstein's baby carriage bouncing down those stairs in *Potemkin*. A film cannot have a spokesman or chorus character to point the moral as in a stage play; that function is assumed by the camera, which is inarticulate. And the absence of spokesmen in the films we remember shows rather eerily that with the cinema, for the first time, humanity has found a narrative medium that is incapable of thought.

3

WHEN speaking of *The Red and the Black*, I said that Julien Sorel patterned his conduct on ideas he had got out of books. In his love-making, for instance, his model was *La Nouvelle Héloïse*, and he was disappointed by not feeling the transports Rousseau had led him to expect. But—on purpose—I failed to mention one book, *the* book that inspired him in all his actions, the book he took for his Bible, that he is immersed in when we first catch sight of him seated astride a roof beam in his father's carpentry shed, oblivious of the mechanical water-saw on a platform a few feet beneath him whose movement he is supposed to be watching and of the shouts of his approaching father. Surprised by his parent in the truant act of reading, he receives a heavy blow that causes the book to fall into the millstream below. A cuff on the head follows, half stunning him. Bleeding and tearful, Julien returns to his place by the saw, but the tears in his eyes are less for the physical pain than for the loss of the book he adores. Jerked to ground level by an iron hook (used for knocking walnuts off a tree), and chased toward the house, sadly he watches the stream—which in fact is the common gutter—that is carrying the book away. It is the *Mémorial de Ste. Hélène*—a semi-spurious collection of thought gems claimed to have been taken down verbatim from Napoleon's conversation during the years of confinement on St. Helena.

In this first telling glimpse, Julien's whole nature and the forces operating it, in a regular action like the saw-mill's, are compressed into two and a quarter pages. We have been shown the play of vectors that determines his direction; what follows will be development and amplification. Before the brief chapter is over, we learn that the cruelly lost volume was part of Julien's legacy from an old Surgeon-Major of Napoleon's armies who had taught the peasant boy Latin and what he himself knew of history, i.e., the history of the Italian campaign of 1796. The Latin and the bit of history are all Julien needs to know to set him in motion. From the veteran he has inherited, besides, the cross of the Legion of Honor, a collection of the bulletins of the Grand Army, and Rousseau's *Confessions*. Those three books and the cross comprise Julien's hope chest.

Multiply Julien and you have the tragi-comedy of France under the Restoration. For lowborn youths fired by ambition, Napoleon was an upstart figure raised to the point of sublimity. His career offered hope and food for thought to every gifted outsider; the fact that the career had been meteoric could not take away its glory or discourage imitation. On the contrary, the precipitous fall of Napoleon from the zenith—did he fall or was he pushed? —added to the bitterness and sense of injustice among the disadvantaged that were in themselves incentives for a new try. Had Napoleon died Emperor rather than prisoner and outlaw, his heirs would have been heirs of his well-cared-for body rather than his soul. There is a vengeful element in Julien's determination to rise. He will *show* the *bien pensants* who wrong his hero that despite them Napoleon lives on, like the hydra; Julien will be a fierce new head poking up among them that mistakenly they will try to stroke.

The Little Corporal who made himself Emperor, rudely gesturing aside the Pope and putting the crown on his own head, is Julien's consuming passion—his only true and lasting one. As tutor in the household of M. de Rênal, he keeps a portrait of Napoleon hidden in his mattress; Mme de Rênal, made aware of the secret, thinks it is a portrait of his mistress, and her instinct is not so wrong. To get ready for the evening when he will need all his courage to seize her hand and hold it, he has devoted an entire day to rereading the *Mémorial*—apparently he has procured a second copy or else Stendhal forgot. Shortly after this episode, he climbs all alone by a goat path to a rocky peak; standing on a huge crag, he spies a bird of prey, a sparrow-hawk, far above him silently wheeling in immense circles and ponders as he watches its still, powerful movements against the sky: "He envied that force, that loneliness. Such had been the destiny of Napoleon; would it one day be his own?" The idea of Napoleon links itself naturally with images of height and isolation, and it is a reprise, surely, of the Napoleonic idea that at the very end of the novel Julien should choose a mountain grotto for his tomb. Death and transfiguration.

This passion of his, amounting to total identification, is a love, however, that dares not speak its name. Wherever he goes among the rich and mean-spirited, he is beset by enemies, his own and the Emperor's—it is the same. He must hear him referred to as the "usurper" (*"l'usurpateur"*) or as *"Buonaparté,"* a pronunciation of the Corsican family name that brings out the wop in him. They will not speak of him as "Napoleon," which is a reminder of his imperial title—only kings and Emperors are known by their Christian names; thus Louis XVI was guillotined as "Louis Capet." In this hateful atmosphere, Julien is obliged to be careful. Wary of M. de Rênal's tours of inspection of the household, he burns the portrait he has been keeping for safety in his mattress. He must read the "inspired book" at night in secret, hiding the lamp under an inverted vase, and speak of his idol with horror, like the rest of the company, whenever the topic comes up. That is the provinces, but the situation is not much better in Paris, in the household of the Marquis de la Mole.

It is clear that Stendhal views the "inspired book" and Julien's raptures over it with amusement. Here is one of the points of difference between author and hero. Julien would hardly think of the *Mémorial* as his "Koran"; that is the author's dry contribution. Stendhal himself was evidently of two minds about Napoleon. Yet if he had to choose, he would certainly prefer the idolators of the Emperor—Julien, the old Surgeon-Major, Fouqué—to his insensate disparagers. The motives of the former seem comparatively innocent.

What Stendhal actually thought of the martyr of St. Helena is not on record, so far as I know. But there is no doubt that he had been drawn to the younger Napoleon, the carrier of the ideas of the French Revolution, dethroner of archaic tyrannies, "breath of fresh air" blowing through the stuffy salon of Europe. Stendhal was no revolutionary, but he was very susceptible to being thrilled. The trees of liberty springing up in public squares in the wake of the victorious armies, the dancing of the carmagnole, like a welcome march, by joyous populations—all this struck a chord of "enthusiasm" to which he always responded. Moreover he had been present during the days of the first delirium. "Bliss was it in that dawn to be alive."

The explosion of joy set off in Milan by the liberating armies is described in the opening chapter of *The Charterhouse of Parma*, so memorably that I do not need to quote from it. Milan is drunk on the elixir of freedom, untasted since the Middle Ages, and Fabrice del Dongo is the child of those intoxicating weeks. I am recalling that paean to put it in the gloomy context of *The Red and the Black*. It cannot be an accident that the history Julien learned, the only history he knew, was precisely the history of that pure, still undefiled period. Here, briefly, the two novels, otherwise so unlike each other, join. From the Italian campaign of 1796, in which the veteran Surgeon-Major had won his *croix de guerre*, the carmagnole dated, having had its fiery baptism four years earlier at Carmagnola, a town of Piedmont occupied by the revolutionaries. The war dance or dance of liberty came home with the armies, and the music, in double time, served the troops of the Revolution as a marching song. When Napoleon became First Consul, he forbade the playing of the tune.

This marked the end of the honeymoon. The tempering of Stendhal's own ardor may date from the Russian campaign, in which he served; there trees of liberty were noticeable by their absence, and the army of freedom had turned into a war machine. Or it may have had more to do with the onset of middle age—he was forty-seven when he published *The Red and the Black*—than with any reasoned reassessment of Napoleon as the bearer of glad tidings to the peoples of the world. It perhaps means something in our context that the young Fabrice's experience of the battle of Waterloo is simply one of utter, aimless confusion; this child conceived in the brio of the victorious Revolution is unaware of being present at a tragedy of epic proportions, unaware, in fact, of being present at a battle of any kind.

But if Stendhal's feelings toward the putative author of the *Mémorial* seem to be reserved, if not ambivalent, in *The Red and the Black*, there can be no question about his clear, objective understanding of the force of Napoleon as idea. This force is shown as a fact, in competition with other facts and hence productive of irony. For Julien Sorel it proves to be a destructive force, but which nevertheless lifts him out of the ordinary, and there is much that is mean and ordinary in him, starting with a small, almost brutishly low forehead that is far from resembling Stendhal's own broad expanse of brow.

In striking contrast, Balzac's hero, Lucien de Rubempré, is noble in appearance; I spoke of his *"beauté surhumaine."* Lucien even has some drops of noble blood in him, on his mother's side. Where Julien with his calculations and retentive memory is the soul of prose, Lucien is a poet. Yet Lucien, too, has the example of Napoleon before him as an *ignis fatuus,* and, like a general, he, too, thinks in terms of conquest. He sees himself, after an undecided skirmish at Angoulême, as the conqueror of Paris, moving boldly from success to success. To his awed friends he is "a young eagle"—a step higher on the scale of predators than the circling hawk that Julien envied. He is "the great man of the provinces" before he has published a word and, of course, a "genius," that is, superhumanly gifted. In the Parisian milieus he enters, Napoleon's star is still visibly beckoning to the obscure and untried. A poorly dressed young man in thick-soled shoes is said to resemble an engraving of a well-known portrait of Napoleon, an engraving which is "a whole poem of ardent melancholy, restrained ambition, hidden activity." Can this be the same portrait as the one Julien owned?

Balzac himself draws the obvious moral; he speaks of *"l'exemple de Napoléon, si fatal au Dix-neuvième siècle par les prétentions qu'il inspire à tant de gens médiocres"* ("the example of Napoleon, so fatal for the Nineteenth century because of the pretensions it inspires in so many mediocrities"). He is thinking of Lucien and his generation, but the remark could serve as an epigraph for both his own novel and Stendhal's—if you grant that Julien is a mediocrity—and an epitaph for their heroes. "Fatal" is indeed the word. Despite differences in tone and in degree of sympathy (Stendhal is fond of Julien), the two stories are eerily alike, to the point where one wonders whether it is not a single book, one and indivisible, that one has been reading, whether in fact all the novels of the century do not refer, each in its own way, to a governing idea—Napoleon.

This last is, of course, an exaggeration. That idea cannot be found in the English novel, which largely ignored him—there are only a few references, scattered here and there. Dickens, when he turned to France in *A Tale of Two Cities*, stopped short with the Terror and the tumbrils; Napoleon was still in the wings, waiting. Wellington unfortunately was no substitute; he was never an Idea on the march, even for his partisans. No ambitious young men in English fiction modeled themselves on the Iron Duke, and it was too late for a generation of budding Cromwells. In a way, I cannot help feeling this as a loss. It may be the reason that nineteenth-century English fiction, in comparison with that of the Continent, seems barren of ideas. There are homiletics and moralizing in plenty but no sovereign concepts. There is no shortage of climbers, but they are ordinary climbers—Lammerses and Veneerings—lacking the divine afflatus. Our own fiction is no better off, with the exception of Captain Ahab, who is obsessed by a personification, though not of the Napoleonic sort. Hyacinth Robinson in *The Princess Casamassima* is a poor excuse for a Leveller.

In Victorian fiction the book that comes closest to having one large governing Idea would be *Dombey and Son*, which I read as a parable of Empire, the Dombey fortune extending tentacles of investment overseas while sickening at the center in the person of poor little Paul and holding somewhere in its clutches Major Joey Bagshot and his servant, called the Native. But Victorian fiction, generally, seems to have missed out through insularity, which was a side-benefit of Empire, on the shaking experience of the century: the fact of seeing an Idea on the march and being unable to forget it—radiant vision or atrocious spectacle, depending on your point of view.

Hegel, at Jena, exclaimed that Napoleon was "an idea on horseback"; being a philosopher, he did not find that antipathetic. A few days later, in a more *terre à terre* frame of mind, he was hurrying to secrete his valuables— manuscript pages of the *Phenomenology*—from the French soldiers. He had already stated in a lecture on history that "A new epoch has arisen. It seems as if the world-spirit [has] succeeded in freeing itself from all foreign objective existence and finally apprehending itself as absolute mind." On the eve of the battle at Jena, which became a Prussian rout, he wrote admiringly of the "world-soul" of the Emperor.

Victor Hugo was harsher in *Les Misérables: "ce sombre athlète du pugilat de la guerre,"* he called the man. It is easier to see what Hugo meant by his curt disparagement than what Hegel meant by his praise. But, between "world-soul" and "Idea on horseback," I suppose Hegel was saying that Napoleon carried the future in himself, and that indeed was what most people thought or feared. To many minds, Napoleon was not just the man of destiny but destiny itself in a tricorne. It was natural, therefore, that youths seeking to be his avatars would feel they bore the stamp of destiny on them, like the visible "stamp of genius" reported to be graven on the foreheads of Lucien himself and of any number of needy young literary aspirants he meets in Paris. These young man were possessed by an overriding idea of their destiny; or, to put it coarsely, they thought they had a "future" and they gambled in their futures like speculators buying next year's wheat shares on the grain exchange.

Such notions were abhorrent to Tolstoy. I do not know how aware he was of the spread of Napoleonic daydreams to the youth of succeeding generations, but he sensed that the glorification of Napoleon was pernicious, whoever was affected by it. One of his main efforts in *War and Peace* is to cut the Idea on horseback down to size. This had nothing to do, I believe, with Russian patriotism—he was hard on the Russian generals too, with the exception of Kutuzov—and if he was more fiercely contemptuous of Napoleon than of, say, Prince Bagration, it was because the man in Napoleon, the parcel of common humanity, had been superseded by an enthroned Idea. The virtue Tolstoy sees in Kutuzov is that, far from claiming to embody in his stout, sleepy person an abstract notion of military genius, he has no particular ideas of strategy in warfare but proceeds by instinct, by a kind of animal cunning, like the fox's. Tolstoy's dislike of the French Emperor, for him inseparable from the tiresome, ridiculous "legend" that he sat for like a portrait, knows no bounds. It even makes him deride the cold Napoleon had on the day of Borodino as being even minimally responsible for the French setback there—a thought that ordinarily would have appealed to him since a cold is a little joke of Nature that can be played on a man of destiny as well as on anybody else. He will not allow Napoleon's cold—inflated to scale by professional historians—to have had any weight at all in the affair.

Tolstoy is not interested in the mighty social forces that may or may not have swept Napoleon and his have-nots to power on a tidal wave of discontent with the status quo ante. He is too pessimistic and, I should say, too acute an observer to expect great changes for humanity in the replacement of one form of power by another. The rapid ennoblement of have-nots into haves by the gift of offices, riches, and titles was only an acceleration of a common social process—the reward system had long been practiced by monarchies. In other words, the revolutionary content of the Napoleonic idea-on-the-march left him cold; he did not believe in its reality. What one finds in *Le rouge et le noir* and *Les illusions perdues* appears to bear him out. Despite the presence of a few lofty spirits— one being an ancient curé—notions of glory and sacrifice, when they are found at all, seem inextricable in most cases from notions of self-advancement, and this cannot be wholly the dampening effect of the Restoration of the Bourbons on young and ardent temperaments.

If Tolstoy took the trouble to polemicize against Napoleon more than forty years after his death, it was not because of any practical harm to be expected from that quarter but because an Idea of him persisted that was injurious to the very act of thought as exemplified in the writing of history. The good reason one might have for such a preoccupation can be clearly seen in the concluding sentences of the article "Napoleon" in the 1911 Britannica: ". . . the great warrior, who died of cancer on the 5th of May, 1821, was thereafter enshrouded in mists of legend through which his form loomed as that of a Prometheus condemned to a lingering agony for his devotion to the cause of humanity." Military prowess had fused with philanthropy. Tolstoy did not look on war as a benefaction and, as a Christian, he could never have sympathized with the picture of a latter-day Prometheus. It is a messianic concept, and there could be only one Messiah; later claimants were necessarily false, a series of vulgar impostors.

He did not care for saviors in whatever shape they presented themselves. As is indicated in *Anna Karenina*, it is enough if a man is able to save his own soul by living for it, which is the same as living for God—the rest will take care of itself. This is the Tolstoyan message, which went through various stages but did not really change. It follows that any hypostasization, of a mental concept such as Hegel's world-soul, or of an aggregate such as the nation, would be to him a criminal impiety. He would have detested the notion of "the century" which we find, writ in shining letters, on page after page of *Les illusions perdues* and, more darkly, in *Le rouge et le noir*. Or more likely he would have snorted with laughter at those Balzacian *littérateurs* haranguing each other about the requirement laid on a book to be "worthy of the century": "If your sonnets are on the level of the Nineteenth century," "Nathan has understood his epoch and responds to its needs," and so on. The last bit is parody, meant to be funny, but the rest is delivered straight, apparently with Balzac's concurrence, as though he considered that a century was an actual living entity with a physiognomy and not just an arbitrary tailor's cut applied to the flow of time. He writes "Nineteenth century" with a capital N, as in "Napoleon," thus raising it above all the humble ones that had preceded. As for Julien Sorel's bitter cry—*"O dix-neuvième siècle"* (no capital)—at the end of *The Red and the Black*, Tolstoy would have advised the unlucky youth to look more closely into his own soul rather than outward at a time-myth when seeking to distribute blame.

The very idea of genius would have been scorned by him too, and not merely when attached to Napoleon as a prodigious military brain. I cannot think he ever used the word, unless in derision; it smacked of charlatanism. All those literary young men in Paris cafés and eating-houses with "genius" stamped on their brows like so many window dummies would have seemed a comic spectacle to the outspoken old man, who would not even put up with it in Shakespeare. Yet there was danger in the silly concept that could not be laughed away, and it was the "irrational" Dostoievsky, not the rational Tolstoy, who fully understood this.

The danger was plainly indicated by Dryden, in 1697, when the word as designating an unusually gifted individual was first coming into use, long before there was a Napoleon to flesh it out on the world stage. "Extraordinary Genius's have a sort of Prerogative, which may dispense them from Laws." Dryden was thinking of art and literature, where genius had a license, recognized at any rate in English-speaking countries, to break rules. Slowly or all of a sudden—a historian of language could doubtless trace the development—this license came to be extended to the moral sphere. The freedom of the genius to violate, say, the unities of dramatic convention was accorded to outstanding men in their personal behavior. It was not yet a question of making one's life a work of art, hence beyond the reach of ordinary conventions; that was left to Oscar Wilde, who announced to the U.S. customs "I have nothing but my genius to declare." That his life was a thing of exquisite beauty never occurred to a Julien Sorel, who did not need the sanction of art to behave unfeelingly. For the common horde of geniuses simply the fact of knowing oneself to be superior was sanction enough, whether the sensed superiority was conferred by an artistic talent, an intellectual capacity, or by some other, not fully disclosed gift.

This, precisely, was the case of Lucien de Rubempré, whose poetic promise, never fulfilled, permitted him to abuse the trust of his family, run up bills with tailor and haberdasher, forge checks, and so on. As the "great man" of the provinces, he was entitled to his just due of misconduct; unfortunately for his peace of mind, he lacked assurance of exactly how much was owing him. His own timidity and the poverty of his relations restricted his predations and even made him ashamed of them. He was not fully possessed of *"l'esprit du siècle"* and half recognized laws other than the law of genius.

Julien Sorel is the opposite. His behavior in every particular has the single purpose of demonstrating that he recognizes no law but his own. In an afterword, Stendhal cites the "law of self-preservation" to excuse Julien's selfishness. But the excuse is a weakness in the author, a tribute paid to convention. In the studied particulars of his daily conduct, Julien has shown that he is above that. When Mathilde de la Mole thinks of him to herself as "a man of genius," it is the truculence of his manners, rather than his endowments, that has been the sure sign of election. Far from being a failing, selfishness is a duty imposed on him; as it is a proof of his superiority, he makes no attempt to hide it.

Genius, it turns out, has requirements; it is not just a carte blanche entitling the holder to run up bills for gloves and cravats. Julien, in fact, is thrifty, like a peasant; he cares nothing for externals and by preference wears his ecclesiastical black. If the Marquis de la Mole prefers to see him in the evenings in a blue coat, he will have to pay for it. The requirements of genius, for Julien, are inward and take the form of a strict duty to the self. In the outer world, he is constantly testing and "proving" himself, but this is not done for the benefit of others. Certain acts must be performed if he is to be true to his Idea. It is at such moments of testing that he turns to his "rule of conduct," the *Mémorial*. Yet the duty summoning him has nothing to do with conscience, and the acts he performs at its order have the character of rites. The gardener's ladder, even though chained down, tells him that he must use it to mount a second time to Mathilde's bedroom; that is the procedure enjoined on him here, as at Mme de Rênal's. As the affair reaches the next prescribed stage, he is like a priest moving from the Epistle side to the Gospel side, or, more precisely, like someone compelling himself to walk on the cracks of the sidewalk or to step over them as the case may be. None of Julien's acts is done from inclination. They are exercises in personal magic.

Now exactly the same can be said of Raskolnikov in *Crime and Punishment*, the last of a line of fictional heroes fathered by the great Napoleon. Raskolnikov does not *want* to kill the old pawnbroker, any more than Julien wants to seize the hand of Mme de Rênal. He forces himself to it, and not from mere desire for her money; by itself, that would be a vulgar motive, a motive anybody might have, given need and opportunity. He does it to test himself, to prove a thesis he has fully accepted in thought and embodied months before in an article: "that there are certain persons who . . . have a perfect right to commit breaches of morality and crimes and that the law is not for them." You will recognize the doctrine even in Russian clothes: "Extraordinary Genius's have a sort of Prerogative, which may dispense them from Laws." By a peculiar twist, already visible in Julien, the "may dispense" has turned into an imperative: "*must* dispense." The student Raskolnikov has the duty of killing the old pawnbroker *if* he is a superior individual. If he is not, there is no obligation.

In his article he has given the hypothetical example of Newton. If Newton's discoveries could only have been made known through the sacrifice of the lives of a hundred men, then "Newton would have had the right, would indeed have been in duty bound to *eliminate* . . . the hundred men for the sake of . . . the whole of humanity." Evidently the cases are not identical. Raskolnikov has made no eminent scientific discovery whose publication would be facilitated by an axe-murder. He is aware of that, yet he is desperately poor, the landlady is dunning him, and he has convinced himself that, apart from personal motives, eliminating an old usuress who has done nothing but evil to her fellow-creatures would be a service to humanity. This benefaction will place him securely among the "extraordinary men" capable of saying a "new word," and the act ought to be no more repugnant to him morally than crushing a louse.

Alas, his being numbered among the extraordinary men has come to depend on his willingness to put the theory he has voiced into practice. Had the idea not presented itself to him and the old woman not been so *logically* available as a subject for experiment, he would still be free. Once the idea has got into his head, he will be a coward to fail to carry it to swift execution. In reality, however, he procrastinates. And here, as was never the case with Julien, there is a struggle of conscience. A strange sort of contest because there are two struggles, really. On the one hand, his good self shrinks in horror from doing "a thing like that," as he calls it almost incredulously on the very first page. On the other, the usual roles are reversed: duty is compelling him to kill the old woman, while his weaker self resists, begging to be let off, to be given a little more time, and so on. He will let circumstances decide for him, he concludes. Yet, as always happens, the longer he dallies, the less ready he is, and the more craven he feels himself to be in the face of an inexorable judge. As Jean Valjean expressed it, in very different conditions, in *Les Misérables*: "To be happy we must never understand what duty is; once we understand it, it is implacable."

Raskolnikov, who has no thought of happiness—happiness is for the ordinary—understands that he will never be at rest till the self-enjoined deed is done. At no point does the crime attract him, not even as sheer idea (duty is unattractive), and, significantly, he never takes the slightest pleasure in picturing the results: how generously he will spend the money, how he will be able at last to face his landlady, stop doing stupid translations for pay. . . . When he steels his nerve for a "rehearsal" of the crime, he is taken aback to find himself in a bright sunny room with geraniums and everything clean and polished; the discrepancy between the pawnbroker's shining flat and his hideous project confuses him, until he is able to reconcile the two by saying to himself, "It's in the houses of spiteful old widows that one finds such cleanliness," as if recalled with sudden relief to his thesis.

Nevertheless, returning to his lodging after the "rehearsal," he feels, says Dostoievsky, like a man condemned to death. He commits the murder, finally, to be done with it, to get it over with, so that he can be left alone. Indeed when he climbs the stairs in the tenement house that are leading him to his mission, he seems to have forgotten why he is doing it; he has lost contact with the wider doctrine that to the superior man everything is permitted and is only putting one foot senselessly before the other, still hoping for a reprieve. In his confusion he overlooks most of the victim's valuables and buries the chamois purse he took from her under a stone. At that moment it occurs to him that he does not know what is in it. " 'If it all has really been done deliberately . . . if I really had a certain and definite object, how is it that I did not even glance into the purse . . . ? . . . And I wanted at once to throw into the water the purse together with all the things which I had not seen either . . . how's that?' " He has duly committed the murder, but the purpose of it has eluded him, cruelly slipping from his grasp.

His crime has been a "fearful burden" weighing on him for months, from the instant of its conception, and he of course experiences a momentary lightness when "It," as he has been calling it, is off his weary shoulders. But the sense of oppression quickly returns, and soon he is flirting with the hope of being detected, feeling impulses to confess, that is, to deposit the burden with the police, who as professionals will maybe know how to handle it. At the same time he is telling himself that "it is not a crime." In a feverish excitement he cries out to himself: "I didn't kill a human being but a principle!" And he thinks that he "will never, never forgive the old woman"—who, having turned into a principle, is evidently responsible for everything.

In sum, like Julien, Raskolnikov has been gripped body and soul by an idea. With Julien, the idea can be roughly equated with ambition. It includes but is not circumscribed by the intention of rising to the top, scaling the peaks of society. And, despite appearances to the contrary, he is successful in his aim, though at the cost of being guillotined. In prison, waiting for execution, he tells himself *"Je suis isolé ici dans ce cachot, mais je n'ai pas vécu isolé sur la terre; j'avais la puissante idée du devoir"* ("Here in this cell I am isolated, but I have not *lived* in isolation on the earth; I had the powerful idea of *duty*"). And he is right in his feeling of triumph. He has distinguished himself, made an indelible mark on his surroundings, as the marble-encrusted mountain sanctuary housing his remains will testify for a great many years, perhaps centuries, to come.

The idea possessing Raskolnikov is ambitious in another sense. He will eliminate an old usuress for the sake of humanity at large. In robbing her, he will also be settling a claim of humanity—the claim of the deserving poor against the undeservedly rich. He expects no glory in return, only the knowledge in his own heart of being equal to the conception he started with, that of the extraordinary individual superior to the rule of law. But—the duty laid on him being weightier, encompassing more than the mere recognition of the self—the result is a total failure. Not the slightest benefit accrues to humanity from his murdering two women (he is obliged to kill her sister too), and the point he wished to prove fails to be made, owing to his inner vacillations, which betray him as not being "up" to the requirements. By ordinary standards, his reluctance to commit the crime would show that he was *better* than he had thought, but those standards, self-evidently, cannot be Raskolnikov's. Dostoievsky, however, has other views; he intends us to see that his hero is better than he knows. Indeed, the punishment of the title consists in Raskolnikov's being forced to come to terms with this humiliating discovery. Yet the author is too considerate, that is, too respectful of Raskolnikov's pride, to show us a conversion taking place. That is withheld from view, kept for another story, as Dostoievsky says at the end. At the close of *this* story, Raskolnikov has begun his atonement, but his reasoning does not yet match the new man he will become.

It will be no surprise to you to hear that on Raskolnikov's list of extraordinary men who were also criminals the familiar name of Napoleon figures. On that honor roll are leaders and legislators who "transgressed the old law" in order to make a new one and shed innocent blood in the process—that is only to be expected, Raskolnikov argues. Otherwise it would be hard for them to get out of the common rut; "and to remain in the common rut is what they can't submit to, from their very nature . . . and to my mind they ought not to submit to it." This conversation, prompted by Raskolnikov's old article, which has unexpectedly come back to haunt him, takes place a week after the double murder, and, though it is a social occasion, an examining magistrate "happens" to be present. With a pair of dreadful winks, the magistrate, Porfiry Porfirovich, wonders whether Raskolnikov, a quite extraordinary young man to all appearances, would bring himself to put his theory into practice. Raskolnikov contemptuously evades the question: "If I did I certainly should not tell you." Porfiry Porfirovich insists that he is speaking from a purely literary point of view. The conversation continues. Then, from a corner of the room, comes the voice of a disagreeable acquaintance: "Perhaps it was one of these future Napoleons who did for Alyona Ivanovna last week?" Raskolnikov does not answer and after an angry look around him turns to go.

At this moment it is obvious that his goose is cooked. His article, taken together with his generally suspicious behavior, has done for him. Though the magistrate, rather frighteningly, seems to be in no hurry to confront him, Raskolnikov knows that it is just a question of time before he is caught in a net mainly of his own fabrication. The memory of his ineptitude fills him with self-hatred. Taking stock a few hours later, alone in his garret room, he whispers to himself in despair, appalled at his past temerity. "And how dared I, knowing myself, knowing how I should be, take up an axe and shed blood!" A thought brings him to a standstill. "No, those men are not made so. The real *Master* to whom all is permitted storms Toulon, makes a massacre in Paris, *forgets* an army in Egypt, *wastes* half a million men in the Moscow expedition and gets off with a jest at Vilna. And altars are set up for him after his death, and so *all* is permitted. No, such people . . . are not of flesh but of bronze!" And he gives a wild laugh, picturing Napoleon creeping under an old pawnbroker's bed.

What has happened is that the distance between himself and "the extraordinary men" has been swiftly widening. Now it has become a terrifying gap, across which he stares back, horror-struck, at Napoleon. And by a stroke of irony this has occurred at the very point when he has been called upon, in a room full of curious listeners, to explain the theory he had stated in his article—an article which, so far as he had known until that instant, had never been published. Yet there it is, and Porfiry Porfirovich has read it, two months before.

Confronted with his theory, like a flesh-and-blood witness, and comparing it with his own behavior during and after the crime, he measures the immense space yawning between. His reaction, perhaps not strange, is pure hatred of Napoleon. The scorn boiling up in his wild, insensate laugh at the picture of the Emperor creeping under an old woman's bed, though aimed at himself, at the absurdity of any comparison, spills over on Napoleon with blistering effect. By imagining the great man under a bed, on all fours, he reduces him to a creeping thing, a louse (his own word later) like himself and the rest of the race. Disconnected thoughts of Egypt, the pyramids (i.e., the monumental), add venom to his merriment. His hatred is double-edged, half for himself and half for the "genius" who encouraged him. With the mocking stress he lays on certain key words ("Master," "forgets," "wastes," "all"), he is taunting Napoleon for his crimes—the very crimes that a few hours before were the slide-rule or gauge of his now loathsome greatness.

In that tirade, a little more than halfway through the novel, an idea is murdered, shockingly, before our eyes. From this point on, Raskolnikov's theory ("no barriers") is dead for him. He has strangled it and tossed it aside, contemptuously, and he has stuck pins into the waxen figure of Napoleon, which bleeds wax blood. Raskolnikov is not yet ready to subject himself to the moral law, but he has no compunction now in subjecting Napoleon to it.

This is not the final word we hear here of Napoleon and the all-is-permitted theory, inseparable companions, but, when next mentioned, they are spoken of histori-

cally, as relegated to the past. When Raskolnikov con-
fesses the murders to Sonia, he tries to explain his reasons
to her. But he has difficulty reconstructing them. He has
to think back and query himself. Finally he decides. "I
wanted to become a Napoleon, that is why I killed her. . . .
Do you understand now?" "N-no," answers Sonia. He
tries again, mentions Toulon, Egypt, becomes incoherent.
"Well, I . . . murdered her, following his example. . . .
Perhaps that's just how it was." "You had better tell me
straight out . . . without examples," she says. Then he
suggests that he did it from need, for his career, to make
himself independent. Sonia is still not satisfied. At last he
thinks he has it: ". . . for the first time an idea took shape
in my mind which no one had ever thought of before me,
no one! . . . I saw clear as daylight that not a single person
living . . . has had the daring to go straight for it all and
send it flying to the devil! I . . . I wanted to *have the daring*
. . . and I killed her. . . . That was the whole cause of it!"

In other words, Napoleon has taken a back seat. He is
of no importance. Raskolnikov himself is the sole cause.
And that, as far as I know, is the last appearance in fiction
of Napoleon as ruling idea. After this, if we meet his
avatars, immersed in the *Mémorial* or joying in his
crimes, it will be in a madhouse.

4

You could say that *Crime and Punishment* was a novel about the difference between theory and practice. Well, if you were a philistine, you could. *The Possessed*, too, deals with advanced ideas and the effects of applying them to life. It does so on a wider scale, and without any reassuring suggestion that to try to implement them is to see them refuted. In the earlier book there was just one theory, Raskolnikov's, which he fails to prove, owing to his own half-heartedness in applying it—an indication of a possible weakness in the theory itself. In *The Possessed*, there is a whole band of theorists, each possessed by a doctrinaire idea, and a whole innocent Russian town to practice on. But in the outcome there is no divergence between idea and reality; in most cases theory and practice have fused, which is what makes the novel so frightening. The exception is the superannuated old liberal, Stepan Trofimovich, an idealist in his writings and something more abject in his daily conduct; such a man can hold no terrors for his fellow-citizens.

It is possible to see *Crime and Punishment* as a prophecy of *The Possessed*. There is the seed of a terrorist in Raskolnikov, which cannot come to fruit since he lacks a prime essential: organization. He is isolated, and his having a devoted mother and sister who bring out the "good" in him makes him feel all the more cut off. He appears to believe in socialism, yet his only friend, the former student Razumihin, is a conservative and disquietingly thick with functionaries of the law. A minor figure, Lebezniatikov, is lumped together with Raskolnikov by a spiteful person as one of a pair of "notorious infidels, agitators, and atheists." Lebezniatikov, who keeps talking about a commune and regards Sonia's being forced into prostitution as "a vigorous protest against the organization of society," is certainly a socialist, but Raskolnikov, who has no time for idiots, consistently gives him a very wide berth. He is reserved, proud, and unsociable and, despite his boldness in theory, never had any plan to commit more than a single murder (the second was unplanned and regretted), obviously not a chain of crimes. A final liability is the difficulty he has in making up his mind.

In *The Possessed*, all these deficiencies are made up. There is determination in Pyotr Verhovensky, an organizing gift, complete absence of scruple. He thinks large, in sweeping arcs, not one faltering step at a time. He is highly sociable, almost convivial, has no pride; when we first meet him, he is described as "an ordinary young man, very lively and free in his manners but nothing special in him." He is constantly paying visits in the town's highest circles but he has other calls to make too. At the direction of a mysterious "Committee" somewhere abroad, he has set up a "quintet" of inconspicuous citizens, each and all inhabited by ideas. These obscure men are chords he knows how to strike at the right moment in a revolutionary overture of his own authorship. The ideas that possess them can be turned to his purposes regardless of intellectual sympathy or of pooling for a common aim. Making up the "quintet" are five one-track minds bent on separate versions of revolutionary doctrine, but for the purpose divergences do not matter, any more than between the first violin and the kettle-drum. The important thing is that each instrument know its cue. And they can function as instruments in Pyotr Verhovensky's diabolical concert because each has merged with an idea; they *are* ideas, so to speak, without ties to anything material, which might serve as a deterrent. Self-persuaded, they need no persuasion. As incarnate ideas, they have lost the power of thought, which may seem paradoxical till you reflect on it. These ordinary men, including fathers of families, have turned into syllogisms, and a syllogism cannot think but merely goes from A to B to C by a rigid track of inference.

The devils of the Russian title are not the quintet, nor Kirillov, nor the young ensign, Erkel. The devils are the ideas in possession of them that have made them into automata. The only demon is Verhovensky, who believes in nothing, has no ideas or principles. If he is an Idea, which I wonder about, it is an idea without specific content, a principle devoted (but not dedicated) to destruction. Dedication is not his style.

He is aware of a lack in himself, which is why he turns to Stavrogin. The nucleus needs a center, and he himself cannot be that, for he is not within but without—a manipulator and strategist. The Byronic figure of the young nobleman appeals to him. His remarkable mask-like beauty, as of Death-in-Life, almost casts him for the central role in Pyotr Stepanovich's Apocalypse. Or, to put it in more practical terms, from what Pyotr has heard of his exploits in the town, he perceives that he can find a use for him: Stavrogin may be able to supply the charisma that is wanting, the seductive spark of the inhuman. Pyotr himself is inhuman enough, but on a lower level of being, as he knows. He is infernal but cold, sharp, precise, business-like. The very fact that he is greedy to make use of Stavrogin, once the possibility has occurred to him, is typical of the economics of his mind. "You will be the leader, I will be your secretary," he tells him at one point, showing as concise a grasp as Stalin's of where the levers of power in revolutionary politics lie. And later, in great excitement: "You are the leader, you are the sun and I am your worm." It is no shock to see him fawning, but his excited state would be quite out of character if he were not carried away by the vision of what he can *do* with Stavrogin.

Verhovensky can find a use for everything, not just the enigmatic vagaries of Stavrogin, but every failing, every tic in the community. These are handles he can coolly pull to initiate action, and the ideas of the quintet, which resemble tics, are among the handles he has practiced with. There is the theory of Shigalov, a man with long ears like a donkey's and a philosophy of despair to match: his final gloomy solution of the social question is "the division of mankind into two unequal parts. One-tenth enjoys absolute liberty and unbounded power over the other nine-tenths." There is the thought of the miserly Liputin, a domestic despot and Fourierist who believes in the "social harmony" and gloats at night over visions of a future phalanstery: he has come to the conclusion that, as the necessary massacre of 100 million persons would take no less than thirty to fifty years to achieve, maybe emigration is the answer.

Those two are adherents of Verhovensky's quintet, but he has many other instruments in the town, sometimes unknown to themselves, for example, the provincial governor's wife, Yulia Mihailovna, who has become so enamored of the new ideas she imbibes from him that she has virtually converted her salon into a revolutionary cell, arousing jealousy in the other ladies. There is Kirillov, a disciple of Feuerbach and believer in a new man-god, who has resolved to commit suicide in order to free other men from the superstitious fear of death. This could not suit Pyotr's hand better, since Kirillov gladly agrees to donate his suicide to the cause, leaving the time of it to Pyotr to fix. It will be timed just right to cover the murder of the brooding Slavophil Shatov, who has broken with the "Society" and whose execution as a spy has been voted by the quintet.

Fedka, the convict, no social idealist, is another of Pyotr's agents. His need of a passport enrolls him initially, and a gift of money assures his following through. With Stavrogin's tacit consent, he will murder a drunkard posing as an army captain, who has got tired of distributing leaflets for the cause, and the fellow's demented crippled sister, whom Stavrogin has secretly married. Even before this, Fedka will undertake another commission, to rob and desecrate an especially venerated icon, along with a confederate—no ordinary criminal but a quintet member—who will commit the ultimate blasphemy of placing a live mouse in it. Coming on top of other indignities, this outrage leads to the district governor's having a nervous breakdown and leaving town for Switzerland. But before his nervous illness is recognized and he is deprived of his functions, this mild bureaucrat has had some striking factory-workers flogged—an error the town will pay dear for.

The fever of organization is such that there is no act that does not lead to something else. Sometimes the hand of Verhovensky is discernible; sometimes not. The vanity of the writer Karmazinov leads him to pronounce an absurd farewell to his public entitled *"Merci"* at the benefit fête for the governesses of the province, and this oration is a contributing cause of the general disorderly uproar that evening, which leads to fires being set. We know that Pyotr did not suggest the topic of the oration—indeed, having been shown the text, he remembers the title as *"Bonjour."* Yet we feel that he was somehow behind the governesses' fête—did he slyly urge the charitable idea on Yulia Mihailovna?—behind the invitation to Karmazinov, who has already demonstrated what a fool he will be on the platform by his excited, approving interest in the manifestoes that are circulating through the town. And who was the guiding spirit in the benefit committee's decision—catastrophic—not to serve a buffet lunch and champagne to ticket-holders?

There is a terrible sequentiality in all this as in "The house that Jack built." Events pile up, and every slender straw thrown on the heap is arsonous. The town is tinder, ready to ignite at a touch. Of course this is mainly the work of Pyotr Stepanovich, who has prepared the ground. Yet there are times when the alarming incidents seem to have their source in some indefinable larger causality. Moreover such implacable sequiturs are not usual in Dostoievsky, where normally there is room for the arbitrary, the *non*-sequitur. Here the only non-sequitur is the unexpected arrival of Shatov's wife, and this is also the only episode that has *no* effect on things to come. It is as though the reasoning process going on in the characters' heads had been copied by outward events, which seem to be obeying Aristotelian logic with never an undistributed middle term. The implacable sequiturs may be comical, too, since the chain of logic, inevitably, is made up of both large beads and small beads, so that if an end-result is a very small bead—the governor in a Swiss rest-home—it is grotesquely out of proportion with the horrors that had led up to it.

Much of this appearance of logic is due to the device of the supposedly objective narrator used here by Dostoievsky. In *Crime and Punishment*, the reader was mostly inside Raskolnikov, listening to his thoughts. In *The Possessed*—with the exception of the suppressed chapter, "Stavrogin's Confession"—everything is told from the outside, by a gossipy young friend of Stepan Trofimovich's, who enjoys his confidence as well as that of the governor's wife, so that he is well placed to tell what went on. He draws no moral conclusions, not being qualified to serve as the author's representative; he simply and somewhat excitedly reports, as though setting the facts straight for some visitor who had missed out on that momentous period "among us." The events are related from hindsight, as he has pieced them together, looking back and verifying where he can. And, like anything seen from hindsight, they fit into a clear sequence of cause and effect—the opposite of what we experience with Raskolnikov, whose perspective is toward the future, hence still open-ended. Moreover the narrator of *The Possessed*, in the interests of historical accuracy, feels obliged not to leave out any detail that might complete the picure. Since he is not quite confident, even looking backward, of being able to distinguish what was important from what was unimportant, we get that comical mixture, typical of gossip, of the relevant and the irrelevant. The mountains are confused with the valleys; the whole moral landscape is obligingly flattened out for our inspection.

This unconsciousness of scale on the part of the narrator is one of the delights of the novel. We understand that we can trust his veracity but not always his judgment; some of the opinions he utters echo in our minds more loudly than he seems to expect. For instance, the well-known passage in the introductory chapter: "At one time it was reported about the town that our little circle was a hotbed of nihilism, profligacy, and godlessness, and the rumor gained more and more strength. And yet we did nothing but engage in the most harmless, agreeable, typically Russian, light-hearted liberal chatter." He is referring to the circle around old Stepan Trofimovich and is saying considerably more than he is aware of saying. To Dostoievsky's mind, the little circle, in the last analysis, has been pretty much what rumor said, all the while maintaining a double screen of illusion about itself. Its members are less dangerous than they generally like to think (here the narrator is right) but more dangerous in their frivolity than he is capable of knowing. In lightly dismissing their talk as harmless, he shows an obliviousness of real consequences that marks him for Dostoievsky as a typical unthinking liberal. The circle of idle chatterers around Stepan Trofimovich was dangerous because it prepared the way for the hyper-active circles that sprang up on the cleared ground.

There is no doubt that Dostoievsky meant to pass a stern judgment when he made the "harmless" old liberal the father of Pyotr Stepanovich and the former tutor of Stavrogin. The devils that were loosed on the community were incubated in that muddled, innocent brain, which when put the question cannot even say unequivocally whether or not it believes in God: "I can't understand why they make me out an infidel here. I believe in God, *mais distinguons*. I believe in Him as a Being who is conscious of Himself in me only. . . . As for Christianity, for all my genuine respect for it . . . I am more of an antique pagan, like the great Goethe. . . ." Liberalism is the father of nihilism; it is only a step to Kirillov and his ruling idea of the man-god, and Kirillov at least has the manhood— or god-hood—to act on his crazed conviction.

The town was "ready" for Pyotr Stepanovich and his quintet, which was only the inner circle of activists. There was a less clearly defined outer circle—possibly there were several concentric ones—of adherents to a secret organization referred to as "the Society." And a proof of the town's "readiness" to catch fire was that there were people in it who did not know whether they were members or not. Long after the scare had died down, an elderly Councillor, wearing the decoration of the Stanislas Order, came forward and confessed that for three months he had been under the influence of the *Internationale*; unable to produce evidence for the claim, he insisted that "he had felt it in all his feelings." Earlier, at the height of the strange affair, the quaking Stepan Trofimovich, who has undergone a police search of his rooms, is queried suddenly by the narrator: " 'Stepan Trofimovich, tell me as a friend . . . do you belong to some secret society or not?' . . . 'That depends, *voyez-vous*.' 'How do you mean "it depends"?' 'When with one's whole heart one is an adherent of progress and . . . who can answer it? You may suppose that you don't belong, and suddenly it turns out that you do. . . .' " In his uncertainty, which fear and pompous vanity make a half-certainty, he is convinced that he is going to be taken "in a cart" to Siberia. The chosen few of the nihilist inner circle are, on the whole, uncompromising in their positions, but those who are outside and somewhat envious (i.e., virtually the entire educated population) behave vis-à-vis the terrorists with the wildest inconsistency. Stepan Trofimovich professes to abhor his son's activities—and maybe he does—yet the narrator learns that on his premises the police have found two manifestoes. "Manifestoes!" cries the narrator. "Do you mean to say you . . ." "Oh, ten were left here," the old man answers with vexation.

Rumor and imagination, naturally, add fuel to the fire that the devils have set. In fact it is a question whether Pyotr's vast organization is not largely imaginary, an idea in his mind. This is Stavrogin's suspicion. It has occurred to him more than once that Pyotr is mad, and Pyotr's worship of him, which he finds repulsive, seems to decide the issue. That happens at a peculiar moment, when Verhovensky finally articulates a credo. He has been saying that he is a scoundrel and not a Socialist. "But the people must believe that we know what we are after. . . . We will proclaim destruction. . . . Well, and there will be an upheaval! There's going to be such an upset as the world has never seen before . . . the earth will weep for its old gods. . . . Well, then we shall bring forward . . . whom? . . . Ivan the Tsarevich. You! You!" After a minute, Stavrogin understands. "A pretender? . . . So that's your plan at last!" He himself is slated to be the pretender. ". . . In this we have a force, and what a force! . . . the whole gimcrack show will fall to the ground, and then we shall consider how to build up an edifice of stone. For the first time! We are going to build it, we, and only we!" "Madness," answers Stavrogin. A few minutes later, Verhovensky, pretty much back to normal, is offering to have Stavrogin's wife murdered free of charge. This comes as a relief. It had been almost a disappointment to find that he had a "positive" side, a "constructive" side, after all.

I am willing to accept that Verhovensky is mad, Stavrogin, the child-violator, is mad, the quintet is mad, Kirillov is mad, and that among the founding members of the local "Society" not even Shatov is sane. A clinical finding to that effect would not greatly alter our understanding of the novel. Possession by an idea is a common form of insanity. But did the entire community go temporarily mad—the governor's wife, the governor, Stepan Trofimovich's protectress, who broke with him because he had not kept her abreast of the new ideas, the old gentleman who was sure that he had been under the influence of the Socialist International for "fully" three months? That, too, is not out of harmony, I think, with the impression Dostoievsky wanted to make. The fact that the whole pathological episode, if that is what it was, is viewed from the outside, as though offered to a clinician for judgment, is surely meant to suggest that. As is known, the story was planned originally as a satire on liberal and nihilist ideas, and much that is satirical survives in the final version: the grotesque members of the "quintet," the governor and his wife, Stepan Trofimovich and his domineering sympathizer, the landowner Varvara Petrovna, "a tall, yellow bony woman with an extremely long face, suggestive of a horse." To picture the new ideas as a virulent illness attacking a body politic is classical strategy on the part of a satirist, and the course of the disease is represented here in what often seems a dry, mock-medical vein: predisposing conditions, first symptoms, onset (Stavrogin biting the governor's ear), temporary remission, aggravated symptoms, spread to other parts of the body, subsidence, final recovery.

Once the figures of Stavrogin, Kirillov, and Shatov were developed—they must have been present in germ from the outset—a gloomy religious element began to suffuse the novel, which up to then one could imagine as a sort of Russian *Headlong Hall,* with perfectibilians, deteriorationists, statu-quo-ites contentedly discoursing while Squire Headlong-Stavrogin set a charge of dynamite to his property. Stavrogin, Kirillov, and Shatov brought suffering—unacceptable to satire—into the tale. Not a ray of comedy falls on them, and yet by a miracle, which I think is effected through the "redemption" of Stepan Trofimovich—a half-ludicrous King Lear of the steppes —the antagonistic elements are able to coexist, the satiric metaphor and something like a Slavophil myth of the Passion.

The loosing of the devils yielded a total of five murders, two suicides, one death-by-manslaughter, one death as a result of exposure (Stepan Trofimovich), two other related deaths, the burning down of a considerable area of the town, general damage to property. Pyotr Stepanovich, the author of it all, escapes as though in a cloud of brimstone, by taking the train to Petersburg.

It is clear that Dostoievsky stood in awe of the power of ideas. The most fearful, evidently, in his eyes were socialistic ideas with their humanitarian tinge. And here at any rate he could speak from experience: his having belonged to a group—the Petrashevsky circle—that engaged in discussions of Utopian socialism had taken him to Siberia and nearly to the firing squad. Yet this experience, he believed, had not only taught him a lesson in the ordinary sense ("Stay out of discussion groups"), but had brought about a spiritual rebirth. His dread of the power of ideas combined with a fatal attraction to them; like so many Russian writers then and now, he was drawn to ideas as if to a potent drug. In Geneva, long after he had returned, a new man, from Siberia, he could not resist going to hear Bakunin expound his theories, and he expressed disappointment that Bakunin was not more constructive. In Dostoievsky, ideas may lead those they fasten on to extreme suffering, but they can also be bringers of redemption, the one in fact leading to the other, as had happened in his own case.

Moreover, once an idea has possessed Dostoievsky he seldom lets it drop but continues to examine it from all sides, at the risk of a certain monotony. Thus Raskolnikov's All-is-permitted theory peeps through at intervals in *The Possessed*; it is Stavrogin who expounds it in his atrocious practice but also in words. As a "prince," he has given the "No barriers" concept an aesthetic twist, almost a cool-headed twirl. "Is it true," Shatov asks him, seemingly much worried, "that you declared you saw no distinction in beauty between some brutal obscene action and any great exploit, even the sacrifice of life for the good of humanity?" Stavrogin does not reply.

It is curious to turn from all this dark questioning to the homely English novel of the same time. George Eliot was a great moral writer, but no character in her novels, however thoughtful, would be asking a question like that of another character. It is not that she would have shrunk from such a phrase as "for the good of humanity"; she thought a great deal about our suffering race and clearly felt that it was her duty to devote her professional life to serving it. Besides she had an interest in theories of socialism and was perfectly familiar with abstract thought. With her competence in French and German, she must have read many of the same books that Dostoievsky read. But the kind of questions her characters put to themselves and to each other, though sometimes lofty, never question basic principles such as the notion of betterment or the inviolability of the moral law. Unlike the great novels of the Continent, the English novel is seldom searching, at any rate not on the plane of articulated thought.

I doubt, for instance, that it could ever have occurred to George Eliot to wonder about the validity of mental activity in itself. She could not have pictured ideas as baleful or at best equivocal forces. About the worst ideas can do, in her view, is to encourage a tendency toward headstrongness in a heroine. We see this in *Middlemarch* with Dorothea Brooke, whose determination to be the helpmeet of Mr. Casaubon springs from a fixed longing of her brain. "It would be like marrying Pascal," she says to herself. "I should learn to see the truth by the same light as great men have seen it by." But it is all a mistake, as with Emma's obstinate plans for Harriet in Jane Austen's novel: Mr. Casaubon is no Pascal; his "Key to All Mythologies," to which Dorothea plans to devote her young energies, is a figment of his fussy, elderly brain, an "idea" he once had for a multi-volume work which is simply gathering dust in his head. In a sense, this, like *Emma*, is an education novel: Dorothea has finally grown up when she learns to stop asking her husband about the progress he is making on his master work.

Among George Eliot's novels, the best place to look for an examination of ideas and their influence might be *Felix Holt, the Radical*. On the surface, this short novel has quite a lot in common with the novels I have been speaking of, especially *Crime and Punishment* and *The Red and the Black*. The hero is a Radical of independent mind. He comes from the lower middle class, is poor, indifferent to his dress, often proudly contemptuous in his manner, and ambitious, not for himself but for humanity or, more accurately, for the small part of it he knows. He wants them all and particularly Esther Lyon to be better than they are. He is angered by her reading-matter— Byron and Chateaubriand—by her ladylike ways and taste for fine gloves, all of which are proofs of shallowness. He is a reformer in the public sphere, too, who earnestly desires to improve the lot of working men and believes that the first step must be to win them from the slavery of drink through night and Sunday classes; without education, the working man cannot advance his cause. When we meet Felix, on the eve of a parliamentary election, he is deeply troubled by corrupt electoral practices: above all, the habit of treating in public houses. In short, he is a man of the Left with a number of stubborn ideas that unfit him for practical politics.

Though he is not a religious believer and despises ordinary conventions, he differs from a Raskolnikov in that he would not consider for an instant violating the moral law in order to benefit humanity. In fact this is precisely what estranges him from the Radical politicians he encounters, who have easy consciences in such matters, accepting with a wink the prospect of violence—a little rough-and-tumble—for the ultimate good of defeating the Tory. Felix would never commit a murder, even in the abstract, turning it over in his mind as a theory. Yet in reality it happens to him to kill a man and to be tried and sentenced for it, though his intention was to halt a riot and the blow he struck was not meant to be mortal. Thus he joins the ranks of principled heroes of nineteenth-century fiction who end up on the wrong side of the law: Jean Valjean, Julien Sorel, Raskolnikov, Nekhludov in *Resurrection*, who joins the woman he has wronged—the prostitute Maslova—in the convict gang traveling to Siberia. No reflection, however, precedes the decision that leads Felix unintentionally to take a man's life; an impulse, rather, rooted in his nature, sends him to try to head off the riotous working men who will only damage their cause and other people's property by a drunken spree of violence. In the style of so many other nineteenth-century "new men," he has proudly announced "I am a man of this generation," but what we find in his actions is a simple old-fashioned boy any mother could be proud of—a testimonial to right training.

"If there's anything our people want convincing of," he tells Esther Lyon when she comes to see him in prison, "it is, that there's some dignity and happiness for a man other than changing his station." (By "our people" he means his own class, the working people, not the English nation, I assume.) Of course there is some truth in what he says, but it is a truth that discourages political action. Felix seems to be totally immune to his century, as though he had been vaccinated against the bug of equality. The novel, which ends with him out of jail and happily married (there is even a little Felix), has a lengthy appendix called "Address to Working Men." There the author imagines Felix expounding his political philosophy to a working-class audience: "Now the only safe way by which society can be steadily improved . . . is not by any attempt to do away directly with existing class distinctions and

111

advantages, as if everybody would have the same sort of work, or lead the same sort of life . . . but by the turning of Class Interests into Class Functions or duties." One is grateful for the knowledge that the address *is* imaginary, with the audience's reaction mercifully *un*imagined.

Despite all her learning and her capacious intelligence, ideas for George Eliot are wholesome moral reflections; she does not seem to have suspected that they could possibly be anything but "improving." Tolerance was her great virtue as a novelist; she always seeks to widen, to make common to all, emotions in her characters' bosoms that the reader might be inclined to spurn any intimacy with. I take an example at random from *Middlemarch*, where the pious banker Bulstrode, obliged to face his conscience, at once begins to dodge. "If this be hypocrisy," the author writes, "it is a process which shows itself occasionally in us all. . . ." The effect of such reminders, page after page, is broadening: we are all made of the same stuff, we have to acknowledge. And, side by side with the injunction to look in the mirror, a general cure is suggested whose name is unselfishness. This is the single thought urged on us by her novels. It is stated explicitly over and over and driven home by telling examples. Mr. Casaubon is selfish, Rosamond Vincy is selfish, her brother Fred is selfish, Tom Tulliver is selfish, Harold Transome is selfish, Esther Lyon starts out to be selfish but is saved in time by Felix Holt. On the other side of the ledger, Maggie Tulliver is unselfish, Mary Garth is unselfish, the Dissenting minister Rufus Lyon is a pillar of unselfishness, Dorothea Brooke is headstrong yet capable of self-sacrifice.

The limitations of this urgent central idea may explain why George Eliot's "good" characters are so unconvincing, even when she tries, as with Felix Holt and Will Ladislaw, to give them a rough edge that might make them complicated to know socially. Her selfish characters are far more persuasive since we are forced to recognize ourselves—or part of ourselves—in them. Thus the virtue of tolerance we are called on to exercise by this writer at her fullest and best has no work to do with the characters we are instructed to admire and to imitate. If George Eliot fails, even in *Middlemarch*, to be a very great writer, this, I think, is because of an intellectual deficiency. The division of central characters into self-seeking and non-self-seeking is inadequate as a key to understanding. In *Felix Holt*, for example, it tells us nothing about the Radicalism that is presumably the subject of the story, and what we get is something strangely like a less ponderous, more charming *Romola*, in costumes of the post-Reform Bill period.

Dickens knew that an idea can be dangerous. Unlike George Eliot, he was familiar with the hold of abstractions on human flesh and blood; it is not surprising that

Dostoievsky read him with eagerness and perhaps learned from him. Still, the incubus or succuba preying on Dickens' people is usually nothing clearly identifiable as a theory or concise program. The great case to the contrary is Mr. Gradgrind in *Hard Times*. From almost the first page, we see how the utilitarian doctrines that have taken possession of his brain are blighting the natural life of his family, how they wither any hope of instruction in the model school he has set up in Coketown. Here he is, in the schoolroom, lecturing the schoolmaster. "Now what I want is, Facts. Teach these boys and girls nothing but Facts. . . . Plant nothing else and root out everything else. You can only form the minds of reasoning animals upon Facts. This is the principle upon which I bring up my own children, and this is the principle upon which I bring up these children. Stick to Facts, Sir!" Then: "Girl number twenty . . . Give me your definition of a horse." Sissy Jupe is too frightened to say anything. "Girl number twenty unable to define a horse!"

Mr. Gradgrind's close friend and business associate is Mr. Bounderby, who has his own *idée fixe* and global explanation, "The turtle soup and the gold spoon. And the venison." It is apparent that these two upholders of the social order are mad, just as mad as the terrorists of *The Possessed*. The reader is meant to understand that Gradgrind and Bounderby are dangerously insane and that at the same time they are perfectly normal, that is, that many other people share the maniacal ideas they express. Bounderby is a wicked bounder, but Gradgrind is not altogether a bad man—a philanthropist, even, according to his lights; he actually has *girls* in his school.

It seems odd at first glance that the idea that has got hold of Mr. Gradgrind should be named by him "Facts." The nature of an idea, surely, is to be abstract, i.e., the polar opposite of the concrete, of the plurality of facts, living and dead, each different from the next, that the world consists of. But we soon understand that Mr. Gradgrind's facts are peculiar, not like the ones we know. Here is a definition of a horse, given by a boy pupil, that he is able to commend: "Quadruped. Gramnivorous. Forty teeth, namely twenty-four grinders, four eye-teeth, and twelve incisors. Sheds coat in the spring; in marshy countries, sheds hoofs, too. Hoofs hard, but requiring to be shod with iron. Age known by marks in the mouth." This sounds like the idea of a horse rather than the fact of a horse. It is as though a drawer labeled "Horse" containing miscellaneous pieces of information, dried and filleted for better storage, had been obediently opened in the filing-cabinet that constitutes the star pupil's mind. The dehydrated facts Mr. Gradgrind favors add up to a fleshless abstraction—horse in general.

The reason for this curious taste of his is evident in his

character: he insists on being in control. And here something of importance for my subject emerges. Ideas are utilitarian. They have a purpose. They are formed in consciousness with a regulatory aim, which is to gain control of the swarming minutiae of experience, give them order and direction. That is Mr. Gradgrind to a T. He believes in education and the extension of knowledge. He wants to see laws formulated for every department of life that will push back the ever-shrinking areas of ignorance, light up dark corners with modern illumination, keep the streets of the mind patrolled. In the interests of thoroughgoing enlightenment, he has forbidden the reading of "idle story-books" in his house. "Idle imagination," he and Bounderby have concluded, is the chief obstacle to the establishment of reason's rule in the young.

Well, it is natural that he should be hostile to novels and natural, in turn, that the novel should be hostile to him, even when it happens that he is not a bad man and means well. If we take Mr. Gradgrind as representing in caricatural form not just his own utilitarian school of thinking (based, after all, on the greatest good of the greatest number) but the mental faculty that is continuously active in formulating ideas, laws, generalizations, then we can look on the novel, which is wedded to minutiae, as his sworn enemy. All art, of course, objects to the continuously active Mr. Gradgrind, but the novel is best armed to do battle with him in that it appears to have one foot in his camp because of the mass of particulars, resembling his "Facts," that it mobilizes for its own purposes.

But it is a strange conflict, with long truces, and often looks like a mere family quarrel. I mean that the novelist's effort—any artist's effort—to impose shape and form on that mass of particulars while maintaining their distinctness has something in common with the mind's will to absolute rule through the synthesizing process. They are similar but they are not the same. The artist's concern (and especially, I should say, the novelist's) must be to save the particulars at all costs, even at the sacrifice of the perfection of the design. An idea cannot have loose ends, but a novel, I almost think, needs them. Nevertheless, there is enough in common for the novelist to feel, like Dostoievsky, the attraction of ideas while taking up arms against them—most often with the weapons of mockery.

We tend to suppose that most novelists take the field against particular ideas, like Dickens in *Hard Times*, that only a few—say, Tolstoy and Lawrence—show an innate angry suspicion of ideas per se, as though the tender living tissue in their care needed protection from the rampaging will to abstraction. Yet even in celebrated victories over specific sets of ideas (Voltaire's disposal of Leibnitz in the person of Dr. Pangloss—"If this is the best of possible worlds, what then are the others?"—Orwell's disposal of Stalinism—"All animals are equal but some are more equal than others"), there is a certain overkill, as though the work were being enjoyed for its own sake. I believe this is always the case, that the tension is always there, except where the novelist has never felt the fascination of ideas, and this, until our own time, has been rare.

I said just now that the novelist's concern must be to save the particulars, and perhaps this needs a little explanation. Even when he shows vast social forces in motion (like Victor Hugo or Manzoni or Tolstoy), the novelist's care is for individual destinies, and it seems to be proper to the novel that they should be small destinies. Not the kings and noble men of the tragic theatre or the witty bloods of comedy but Renzo and Lucia, Tess, Jude, Stephen Blackpool, Felix and Esther, Cosette. None of these poor sparrows "fits" into the overall social framework, and if they have a place in a larger scheme, it can only be God's, which is unknowable. "The President of the Immortals had finished his sport with Tess." Now this habit of concern for the small predisposes the novelist to distrust generalization, i.e., to champion Dobbin against the gramnivorous quadruped. The position, however, is not simple. As we have seen, there appears to be an affinity between Ideas and facts, both Mr. Gradgrind's kind and the other, that is, between the lofty and the very small, as though in the novel they grew together, like the red rose and the green briar in the ballad.

Besides, in the past, if the novelist's mission to teach and improve inclined him to Mr. Gradgrind's side, his common sense—a highly necessary faculty for the novelist, which I have neglected to mention until now—and his powers of observation led him to despair of *any* recipes for improvement or else to fall back, like George Eliot, on simple housewifely stand-bys: Forget Self and Think of Others.

Today there is no longer a dilemma. Ideas are held not to belong in the novel; in the art of fiction we have progressed beyond such simplicities. The doctrine of progress in the arts is a hard doctrine, imposing itself even on those who are fervent non-believers. The artist is an imitative beast, and, being of my place and time, I cannot philosophize in a novel in the good old way, any more than I can write "We mortals." A novel that has ideas in it stamps itself as dated; there is no escape from that law.

For a time, about twenty years ago, it looked as if there could be a compromise. Though an author of standing knew better than to put explicit ideas in his novels, they could be there implicitly, and the reader was allowed—as a student, even encouraged—to take them out. "What are Golding's ideas in *The Lord of the Flies*?" "Is there a Manichean split in Faulkner's *The Wild Palms*?" Today all that is quite impermissible. What the author may not put in, the reader may not take out. There must be nothing said or hinted that is remotely subject to paraphrase. In the place of ideas, images still rule the roost, and Balzac's distinction between the *roman idéé* and the *roman imagé* appears to have been prophetic, though his order of preference is reversed.

Nevertheless, there are a few back doors left through which ideas may be spirited in, and some talented authors have found them. One brilliant example was furnished by J. G. Farrell in *The Siege of Krishnapur*, a novel teeming with ideas that is set in India at the time of the Sepoy Mutiny and has an exciting plot as well. Farrell's motto might have been stated thus: If because of ideas and other unfashionable components your novel is going to seem dated, don't be alarmed—date it. *The Singapore Grip*— Farrell's last novel; he was drowned this past summer— carries the principle on to the fall of Singapore in the Second World War: ideas, characters, and setting have a distinct period flavor, that is, they are as solid as furniture and without any touch of camp. A more recent novel, John Updike's *The Coup*, performs a rather similar feat, moving back, as it were, in time via geography: a "developing" African country bristles with ideas, mainly in the head of its hero, a Western-educated native dictator who finishes, still reflective, in exile in the south of France.

was also Alison Lurie's *Only Children*, set in the
rties with the ideas and life-styles of the period. In
.S.A., a special license has always been granted to
Jewish novel, which is free to juggle ideas in full view
the public; Bellow, Malamud, Philip Roth still avail
themselves of the right, which is never conceded to us
goys. In concluding, I might mention an unusual solution
to the problem. This was Robert Pirsig's *Zen and the Art
of Motorcycle Maintenance*, an American story of a cross-
country trip with philosophical interludes—one of the
chief characters was named Phaedrus. Pirsig's device was
simple; he refrained, probably at a financial sacrifice,
from calling his book a novel, and it was listed as a nonfic-
tion title. If the novel is to be revitalized, maybe more
such emergency strategies will have to be employed to
disarm and disorient reviewers and teachers of literature,
who, as always, are the reader's main foe.